RESTORED
SOUL

Affirmed by God's Resilient Love

All Scripture quotations, unless otherwise indicated, are taken from the Holy Bible, New International Version®, NIV®. Copyright © 1973, 1978,1984, 2011 by Biblica, Inc.™ Used by permission of Zondervan. All rights reserved worldwide. www.zondervan.com. The "NIV" and "New International Version" are trademarks registered in the United States Patent and Trademark Office by Biblica, Inc. ™

Scripture quotations marked NKJV are taken from the New King James Version. Copyright© 1982, 1992 by Thomas Nelson, Inc. Used by permission All rights reserved.

Scripture quotations marked "The MSG Bible" are taken from The Message Bible. Copyright © 1993, 1994, 1995, 1996, 2000, 2001, 2002. Used by permission of NavPress Publishing Group.

Scripture quotations taken from the Amplified' Bible,
Copyright © 1954, 1958, 1962, 1964, 1965, 1987 by The Lockman Foundation
Used by permission." (www.Lockman.org)
Definitions are derived from Merriam-Webster Online Dictionary copyright © 2012 by Merriam-Webster, Incorporated

Scripture quotations marked TPT are from The Passion Translation®. Copyright © 2017, 2018 by Passion & Fire Ministries, Inc. Used by permission. All rights reserved. ThePassionTranslation.com.

Interior Design by: https://www.fiverr.com/istvanszaboifj
Asif Cover Design by: https://www.fiverr.com/nirkri
Cover Photo: Orpheusandaphroditephotography.com
Amazon Kindle Press Publishing Platform
ISBN-13: 9781082101076 (Amazon Kindle Press)
BISAC: Religion / Christian Life / Spiritual Growth

RESTORED
SOUL

Affirmed by God's Resilient Love

45-DAY DEVOTIONAL

KIMBERLY MICHELLE FORD

DEDICATION

This book is dedicated to:
every heartbreak,
every moment of abandonment,
& every fear of rejection.

This book is dedicated to:
every tear,
every sleepless night,
& every nightmare of loneliness.

This book is dedicated to:
emotional hurt,
physical pain,
& Unwarranted shame.

This book serves notice to the enemy
that in every way he has tried to break me down to nothing,
The resilient love of my God has
"Restored My Thirsty Soul"

ACKNOWLEDGEMENT

For You

Jessika

CONTENTS
Affirmed by God's Resilient Love

FOREWORD

Apostle Stephen A. Davis

G od loved us and responded by giving; it is His nature. When you misinterpret the nature of God, you misinterpret those who embody Him. When mimicking the love of God, you must remember that you cannot wait for people to perform the way you want them to *before* you love them. The foundation of this book emphasizes this by showing that "God's breath gave soul to a void man." From this quote alone, Minister Ford shows the nature of God, despite the state of man. Through highlighting God's nature to restore a void man because of His unbounding love, we also highlight the importance of surrendering control of who fills our voids. God restores our soul and helps us in our wholeness. Allowing God to fill your voids puts you and your enemy on level playing ground and gives you the advantage. Full restoration will be given with proceeds.

In this devotional, Minister Ford shines a light on the many ways that hardships in life and relationships can cause us to be left feeling void, discouraged, and even soulless. She also points out how we often like to feel invincible in our own right when facing trials. God wants to show himself in your life, and you can't allow others to get in the way of that. It takes faith to get through adversity. We must remember that we can never attempt to proceed forward without faith. You must be prepared for any and everything, and faith is what will help you to overcome adversity. Faith equals balance.

I trust that as you adopt and follow this daily devotional as a part of your journey to restoration, you will be encouraged by the wisdom and strength of Minister Ford to be resurrected - despite the odds. By allowing her hardships and victories to catapult her deeper into God's word, Minister Ford has become a master in the area of healthy souls. As revealed several times throughout her books, Minister Ford has overcome many obstacles in her relationships by continuing to hold tight to God's promises. She strategically processes her pain until she sees those promises manifest in her own life. Minister Ford has dedicated her writings to encourage others who have faced soul damaging hardships and traumas in life. Often the best teacher is someone who has experienced challenges in life and has come out on the other side with a firm grip on their faith. Minister Ford is that someone. If your soul is in need of restoring, allow this 45-day devotional to guide you through the path of acquiring a *Restored Soul.*

Apostle Stephen A. Davis

HE RESTORES MY SOUL...

He restores my soul;
He leads me in the paths of righteousness
For His name's sake.
Psalm 23:3 NKJV

o restore something is to return it to its original *intent*, original *purpose*, unique *glow*, or original *finish*! The word *restore* is synonymous with "refreshing" and "renewing". The term "*soul*" is synonymous with "*breath*". Therefore, when God released His *breath* – He released His *soul*. As we know it, when God first created man, he was an empty shell, void of any life. Then, as God breathed into the nostrils of man, the soul of God inhabited Adam's empty carcass. At that very instant, Adam was born. He sprung up and became a living soul!

We like to think we are invincible at times. Sometimes we ascribe to the belief that we are indestructible. We think this way because as we approach the tragedies and traumas in this life, we believe that we must approach them convinced -- beyond any doubt—that we possess the power to overcome.

Yet, the very thought that we are incapable of being broken is futile. These bodies, (*these vessels*) we journey through life in, are incredibly fragile indeed. With one wrong decision, one accident, one sneeze, one bullet –in one millisecond –the *soul* of God which causes us to exist can again vacate this shell. Then, just like that, again, our once sturdy frame becomes void of all life.

No matter how invincible we desire to be, each of our lives is dependent upon a living soul. Every breath we take is priceless. No matter what obstacles or disappointments we encounter, we must keep breathing.

In the 23rd Psalms, I am persuaded that David desired to articulate his experience as a recipient of God's healing through restoration. David experienced an immeasurable amount of heartache in his lifetime. Like us, he frequently found himself searching for the strength to keep going – to keep believing – to keep breathing. In the 3rd verse, David is demonstrating to us that after heartache, God is faithful to restore our souls. We may find ourselves broken, disappointed, and depressed – searching for the reason to keep going. In that hopeless and broken place, our Father will draw us into His bosom to heal. As a result, through worship in His presence, He returns us to our "original purpose" for breathing. In His presence, He reminds us of the reason He gave us life.

Through the redemptive power of Christ, God relieves us of the burden of sin and shame. He relieves us of anything that would hinder us from experiencing true worship with Him. Our dreams, goals, and pursuits are proven to be very dynamic. We are continually evolving because there is always something new to *become* on the horizon. Still, more than anything else, there is but one paramount reason we are all here. Our primary reason for existence is *to worship Him.*

Interrupted Breath

We have all encountered relationships that have proven to test our ability to "love beyond hurt". Death, abandonment, divorce, betrayal, and rejection are all conventional catalysts of our broken relationships. Those of us who find the courage to do so, we open our hearts, inviting others in to experience the most intimate part of us—our soul. We invite others into our lives to experience the breath of God through us. Then, when they reject or abandon the sacrilege of our being, it is a natural human experience to feel the pain of detachment; pain fueled by loneliness, hopelessness, and emptiness. We can find it so difficult to breathe that it may seem they have taken our souls with them. Even worse, the hurt is so great that some start to believe that this *must* be where life is supposed to end. Sadly enough, some may become so weak they turn suicidal and succumb to the pain of this experience.

Seeking His Grace to Heal

However, God desires that when we hurt, we seek His grace to heal. The bible tells us in 3rd John 1:2 that the Lord "desires to see us prosper and be in good health – *even as our soul prospers.*" God desires that we would prosper in our *reason for existing*. Since our reason for existing is worship, He ultimately desires that we would prosper and thrive in our *worship*.

Beloved, God desires to come into your heart and show you the authentic love you are longing. It has taken me years of abandonment and rejection to learn that His love is all-sufficient. The love I was denied from my parents, the love I craved from ex-husbands or boyfriends, the love I tried to cultivate in friendships – all paled in comparison to the love God has to offer me. Despite who leaves my life or betrays my heart, God's love is always right there. Still, to experience the fulfillment of His love, I've got to be intentional about seeking Him.

Jeremiah 29:13 tells us that we will only *find Him* when we *seek Him* – with our whole heart. His word makes sure to emphasize that we must seek Him with our "*whole*" heart. We give away so much of our hearts to people, especially if we think they are "*the one*". Sometimes, we are guilty of abandoning our kingdom assignments and becoming distracted from purpose when we believe we have discovered real intimacy with another human being. We lose interest in the things that bring us life as an individual. Ultimately, we abandon worship and trade our fellowship with the Father for quality time in fellowship with our loved ones. We have all, at one time or another, been guilty of expecting our lovers, children, and friends to fill our voids of intimacy – instead of relying upon the agape love of the Father to satisfy our thirsty souls.

In the meantime, God is waiting for you to give Him *all of you*. Sometimes, we must surrender to His beckoning by releasing the people who hinder that fellowship for a season...and pursue *Him*. Even when we are in the single-season of our lives, this period is designed to be an amazing time of uninterrupted fellowship with the Father.

In our surrender, we find a closer relationship with Him. In each of our relationship experiences, whether they are good or bad, God desires that we experience Him in the process. Regardless of the outcome, God is always present. Therefore, our ability to love and forgive one another in relationships should reflect the love and forgiveness He has demonstrated to us.

By the end of this 45-day devotional, it is my prayer that your heart will be restored to the state God created it in, *whole*. Our hearts were not designed to withstand the burden of hurt and pain that many of us carry. Many of the diseases we contract in our bodies are the result of our inability to manage the weight of emotional pain and trauma. No matter how much or who you think you have lost, God wants you healed of the hurt. It is His heart's greatest desire that you would be delivered from the bondage of regret that has hindered your ability to LOVE again. Despite the abandonment of others, *He* has not left you. Despite the rejection of those who were supposed to love you, *He* still wants you. You are still His! He wants you to believe and to breathe again.

You will move on from here.

You will laugh again.

You will live again.

God created you to LOVE.

Authentic love never dies; it just lives on in us.

–Kimberly Ford

PART I.

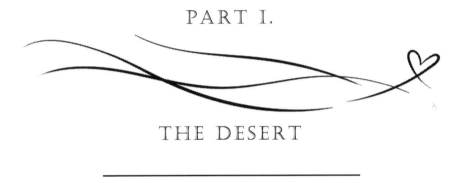

THE DESERT

A Prayer of David When he was in the Desert of Judah
O God, You are my God; with deepest longing I will seek You;
My [a]soul [my life, my very self] thirsts for You, my flesh longs and sighs for
You, In a dry and weary land where there is no water.

Psalm 63:1 Amp.

THE PRAYER OF A WOUNDED SOUL

*H*eavenly Father, Restore my broken soul. You are the great Author and Finisher of my fate. Before you formed me in my mother's womb, You knew me. In You, I was fearfully and wonderfully made. You skillfully crafted and covered me in the radiance of Your Love. Then, You trusted Your work in me and placed me here, in time – the space between You and me. Here in time, my eyes have seen great tragedy. Here in time, my heart has felt great pain. This journey back to You has worn me down. I have come to a place deep down in the valley, and my soul is broken. I'm in a dark place, and I just need somewhere to lay my head and rest. My heart has been trampled and used as a footstool. Some saw its strength and used it to elevate themselves – when they didn't have the power to stand on their own. My heart has been broken and bandaged one too many times. I've run out of bandages, and the scars have outnumbered my tears. I have journeyed on this conquest for love, for so many years. I have traded my wealth and my health for a possible chance to experience it. I have given beyond my ability to deliver. And I have trusted – even when I couldn't understand. But now, Father, I've come to a silent place. The laughter has ceased, and the fun is over. That which I thought would sustain me, has only disappointed me. I couldn't believe it at first, but those who I thought were here to stay, walked (and some ran) away. So, I stand here alone— weak, fragile, and afraid. My fears have multiplied without my knowing it. I don't know what tomorrow holds. I don't trust my own decisions anymore. I have unknowingly invited abuse and disaster into my life and carelessly rejected authentic gentleness. I have foolishly partnered with serpents and regretfully wrestled with the angels. I have freely given the treasures of my heart to thieves but held back my love from my Redeemer. Lord, I can't tell the real from the counterfeit. So now, my insecurities block me from trying at all. Forgive me, Father, for not seeking Your face and following the sound of Your voice. You, Father, have seen my end from the beginning. You have watched me crawling along – trying everything and everyone else. I have reached for everything else except You to fill this hole in my soul. So now, I look to you. I am reaching for you. Where else could I go? Bring me back to a place where I can stand. I trust you to calm the raging sea of my mind. Heal my trampled heart. And, Heavenly Father, restore my broken soul. *Amen.*

Summing it all up, friends, I'd say you'll do best by filling your minds and meditating on things true, noble, reputable, authentic, compelling, gracious— the best, not the worst; the beautiful, not the ugly; things to praise not things to curse. Put into practice what you learned from me, what you heard and saw and realized. Do that, and God who makes everything work together will work you into His most excellent harmonies.

Philippians 4:8-9

The Message Bible

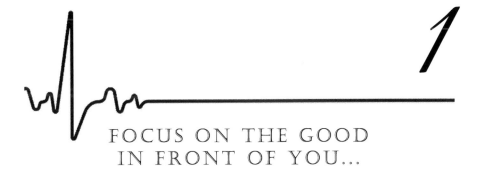

FOCUS ON THE GOOD
IN FRONT OF YOU...

*T*ake a good look in the mirror. What do you see? Is it the you that you want to see? Do you identify with the greatness staring back at you? After you have experienced the heartbreak of a broken relationship, you may begin to wonder, "Was it something I did? Could I have done something differently? Was I good enough?"

Maybe *it was*, in fact, something you did. Perhaps you *could have* done something different. But what good does it do you to hold on to your mistakes and regrets? I've never known them to have any value in our accounts. We will experience many relationships in our lifetime. Our relationship *lessons* are like deposits made into our heart accounts. *Regrets* are like withdrawals. If we continue to hold on to the disappointments in our relationships, we will eventually find ourselves bankrupt. It is wise to take inventory of the relationships you experience and extract a valuable lesson from each of them.

I encourage you to hold on to the lesson and release the mistakes. Looking back at your mistakes in regret will only give you a spiritual cramp. To fully experience the greatness God puts in front of you, you must be fully present. It is impossible to be crying about yesterday and enjoying today both at the same time.

There is still some good inside of you, and God wants you to acknowledge it. For the sake of future relationships, you must first pursue and discover that which is good. You have the right to live and love again. But if you are not looking forward, in the direction of love, you will miss it when it presents itself. Great is His love *for* us and *in* us.

Today's Reflection:

Take a moment here and review the most intimate relationships that have impacted your life. In the rows below, list all of the names of those relationships that resulted in some form of trauma or disappointment for you. This may be a spouse, a close relative, a friend, a co-worker, boss, etc. Beside each name describe the lesson learned from that relationship.

_____

_____

_____

_____

_____

_____

_____

_____

_____

_____

_____

_____

_____

_____

_____

_____

I am absolutely convinced that nothing – nothing living or dead, angelic or demonic, today or tomorrow, high or low, thinkable or unthinkable—absolutely nothing can get between us and God's love because of the way that Jesus our Master has embraced us.

Romans 8:38-39
The Message Bible

LEARN TO LOVE
WHAT'S GOOD FOR YOU...

*E*ven the strongest of relationships are subject to be tested. Even those built on the rock will have to learn how to weather the storm. Still, those tests and storms will determine if the relationship has been built to last a lifetime. If we are brutally honest with ourselves, there are likely some people we wish we could write out of the story of our lives. We may have even prayed for God to remove them. Yet, for some reason, they are still here with us. For some reason, after the deadliest of arguments, they return to us ready and unafraid to love us again. Chances are, you have both forgotten the reason you fought in the first place. These are the relationships God has blessed with longevity. They cause us to grow, mature, and seek a higher purpose. These relationships are good for us because they teach us how to love, forgive, and forget.

But then there are some people we have spent our lives chasing. We may have spent countless hours in prayer asking for the relationship to someway, somehow get grounded. We have shed far too many tears in agony, confused as to why they won't love us back. Yet, the person runs from us, and our tears go unnoticed. We have offered everything we could offer to persuade them to stay. But still, they are determined to *go*. As much as we want them to stay, God is doing you a favor you probably won't understand right now. He knows there is something about them that does not compliment the direction you are traveling in life. There is something about them that will hinder your growth.

So as painful as it may be, embrace the lessons that come from the relationships that test your patience. They really are for your good. Then release the ones that buck like a horse to be free.

Today's Reflection:

What relationship has challenged your personal growth the greatest? In today's reflection, describe some key areas where your character was tested in this relationship.

_____

_____

_____

_____

_____

_____

_____

_____

_____

_____

_____

_____

_____

_____

_____

_____

_____

Forget about what's happened; don't keep going over old history. Be alert; be present. I'm about to do something brand new. It's bursting out! Don't you see it? There it is! I'm making a road through the desert, rivers in the badlands. Wild animals will say, 'thank you!'—the coyotes and the buzzards—Because I provided water in the desert, rivers through the sun-baked earth, drinking water for the people I made especially for myself, a people custom-made to praise me.

Isaiah 43:18-21
The Message Bible

3

FORGET IT... *ALL* OF IT!

woman wakes up each morning and walks into her studio to paint. She dresses in her apron. Then she sits on the stool and turns the page on the easel to a new slate. She picks up the tray of watercolors and paintbrushes. She begins to paint. Each stroke lands perfectly on the canvas, and all the colors seem to fall right into place. She finishes the piece and begins to weep. Each day as she stares at her work, she weeps. She's crying because she can't seem to paint anything new. She awakens each day with the same picture in mind. Therefore, she wakes up each day going through the same routine and repeatedly paints the same image.

It is never easy to let go of the pain from yesterday. Your spouse may have broken your heart. Your best friend may have abandoned or disappointed you. There are hurtful things people have said and done to etch memories on our soul, never to be removed. But when the experiences behind you are so painful that you can't move forward, then it's time to begin with a new canvas and a new paintbrush.

You may have spent countless days, hours, dreams, and nightmares rehearsing the events of your past. Doing so, you are literally painting the same picture over and over again, just like the woman in the studio. Yes, unexpected tragedies may have altered the path of your life. But you do not have to allow your past to impact, dictate, or shape your future. Until you put these experiences behind you, you will not see the new opportunities that stand in front of you today, what you did yesterday shaped today. Only what you do today has the power to shape tomorrow. So, it's time to stop rehearsing yesterday and begin to focus on the choices you make today. You've been given a fresh, clean canvas. Let's paint something new.

Today's Reflection:

It's never easy to imagine the new dynamics of life after the loss of a loved one -- whether it's by divorce, death, or betrayal. Maybe your children have left for college and you are left to redefine your life's purpose. Still, as we struggle to imagine a new life on the other side of disappointment, God reminds us that we must write the vision and make it plain. So today let's paint a new picture of what your "best life" looks like. In today's reflection, try to list up to 20 new things you have never done before. Have fun with it. Then after you've completed the list, rank them from 1-20; with 1 being the thing you will be intentional about doing first and 20 being the last.

_____

_____

_____

_____

_____

_____

_____

_____

_____

_____

_____

_____

_____

_____

_____

Now we look inside, and what we see is that anyone united with the Messiah gets a fresh start, is created new. The old life is gone; a new life burgeons! Look at it! All this comes from the God who settled the relationship between us and Him, and then called us to settle our relationships with each other.

2 Corinthians 5:16-19

The Message Bible

And when you assume the posture of prayer, remember that it's not all asking. If you have anything against someone, forgive—only then will your heavenly Father be inclined to also wipe your slate clean of sins.

Mark 11:25

The Message Bible

4

PAID IN FULL...

orgiveness is like the bridge that we must all cross to enter the land flowing with milk and honey. Birds are chirping, and the sun is shining on the other side. The trees are green, and the grass looks soft. The fragrance of the air that blows, from the other land smells sweet like honeysuckle. Still, no matter how wonderful things look over there, nobody ever wants to pay the toll to cross.

We show up at the bridge called forgiveness, empty-handed, and frustrated. We feel as if somebody, somewhere, has stolen our fare to cross. Somebody raped us. Somebody abandoned us. Somebody brutally abused us. Each time, that same somebody took something from us. That piece of our heart that grants us access to live and love freely. When they took that small bit of us away, we entered a deficit. Somebody owes us! *Right*?

Wrong!! The only person that owes you—*is you*. Yes, someone temporarily damaged a piece of your heart. But that can be fixed. Yes, someone ruined precious years of your life. But those can be restored. What they didn't take—couldn't take – was the God *in you*. And as long as you still have that, they have not taken much at all.

If you don't cancel the debts of those who have hurt you, you will wind up charging these debts to the new people that come into your life.

And as you do so, you will remain at the bridge wishing each person that passes by would pay the toll for you to cross over into abundance.

Do yourself a favor and stop expecting someone else to settle the debts. Nobody wants to pay the price for a crime they haven't committed. God has forgiven them, and now you should too. It's time you cross that bridge called forgiveness and cancel the debts of your past. No matter what happened, the blessing is that you are still standing. When you come to the bridge of forgiveness, you will find that the toll for you to cross was already paid in full.

Today's Reflection:

In today's reflection, we will be transparent about forgiveness. Let's start by answering the question: Who did what? When? And how? How do *you* believe the event was able to happen? Then. in the space below, write a letter of release to the person you need to forgive most.

WHO?	
DID WHAT?	
WHEN?	
WHERE?	
HOW?	

_____

_____

_____

_____

_____

_____

_____

_____

_____

_____

_____

What God did, in this case, made it perfectly plain that His purpose is not a hit-or-miss thing dependent upon what we do or don't do. But a sure thing determined by His decision, flowing steadily from His initiative.

Romans 9:10-13

The Message Bible

5

APPRECIATE
THE EXPERIENCE...

*D*oes the diamond ask for fire, or does the clay ask for the wheel? The diamond, which begins as a dirty worthless rock, is forced into flames for countless days and hours for all impurities to be burned away. After the process, it comes forth as one of the world's most precious stones. Here's another example: clay begins as pure dirt. When wet, it becomes mud. Most people are unhappy if their clothes are soiled and stained with wet *mud*. As the potter mixes clay with water and places it on his wheel, that same mud is molded and sculpted into something priceless. Its uniqueness is unable to be duplicated. It soon becomes a priceless vessel, sometimes being valued at thousands and millions of dollars.

No, you didn't ask for the pain of a broken marriage. No, you didn't ask to experience the death of a child. You weren't expecting to be laid off from your dream job. As you work on forgiving the culprit of your pain, it is essential that you learn to appreciate the experience they forced you to have. Because of that tragedy, you are more robust. Because you were abandoned, you are financially wiser. You were abused. Therefore, you are more compassionate towards others. If it were not for that experience, you would not be where you are today.

It might not seem fair to credit your success to the people who brought you to the lowest places in your life. Who really wants to give credit to the very people who wanted to see you fail? If the truth were being told, your position in the fire was precisely where God needed you to be. To grow and mature spiritually, most times, we must be forced out of our comfort zones. When things are going well, and everything seems high in our lives, we are not passionate or pressured to change anything in it. That doesn't mean you are not entitled to live a life of peace and harmony. It does mean, however, that to get the best out of the tree of life, sometimes it must be shaken.

Today's Reflection:

When we experience trauma, the last thing we are looking for is the silver lining. But today, let's give it a try. In today's reflection, recount the greatest trauma you have experienced. Maybe it happened in your childhood. Maybe it was a broken personal dream. After you have described the unexpected traumatic experience, then pray and ask God to reveal at least one positive outcome from the event.

_____

_____

_____

_____

_____

_____

_____

_____

_____

_____

_____

_____

_____

_____

_____

_____

_____

The race is not to the swift or to the strong,
nor satisfaction to the wise,
nor riches to the smart,
nor grace to the learned
sooner or later, bad luck hits us all.
Ecclesiastes 9:11
The Message Bible

"Staying with it—that's what God requires.
Stay with it to the end.
You won't be sorry, and you'll be saved."
Matthew 24:13
The Message Bible

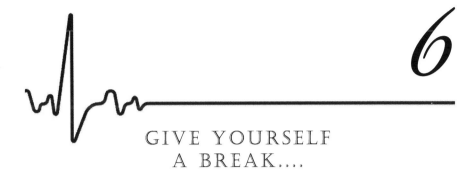

GIVE YOURSELF
A BREAK....

*R*unners on your mark! Runners get set! *GO!!* And he takes off running as fast as he can. He has waited all night for this race. All the other heats have finally finished. He has spent all evening exercising to keep his muscles warm. But now it's raining, and his body begins to stiffen. He is a star sprinter. He was built for this race. Still, he, along with all the other runners, is disappointed with the worst recorded running times of their season. His mother is there alone, sitting in the rain, holding her umbrella. No matter what the weather is, she wouldn't miss a chance to see him run.

He leaves the field, soaked with rain and sweat. Then he heads towards His mother with his bag on His shoulder, and head hung down. "Mom, I've never run so bad in my life. That was a horrible race!" he sulks in disappointment. She looks him square in the face and tells him, "Give yourself a break, you ran!"

I am convinced, no one is exempt from ever having made a mess. Sometimes you just might choose the wrong mate. You might have been the one to make a bad decision, ultimately destroying your relationship. We have all made mistakes inflicting grief on ourselves as well as others. Here is something to consider; if you never allow yourself room to fall, you will never learn how to get up.

Learn to celebrate the fact that you showed up for the race, and you gave it your best shot. However, just because you give it your best shot doesn't mean you will always come home with a shiny medal. You gave that last relationship your best. You did what you thought was best at the time. Still, that didn't guarantee you a place at the altar saying, "I do." Some relationships are like the heats in a track meet, used to determine how ready you are for the finals. They might not end the way you want them to. But give yourself a break, *you ran!*

Today's Reflection:

It takes courage to acknowledge when your actions have led to the failure of a relationship. It's natural to drop our heads in shame and vow to never try again. Sometimes we wonder how in the world did I mess that up? We're left feeling inadequate and like we don't deserve another chance. To move forward, we must first acknowledge our actions, forgive ourselves, and then be affirmed knowing that God still wants what's best for us. In today's reflection, think about a particular mistake you have made that had a detrimental impact on your life. Acknowledge your error. Then end the reflection by writing a letter of release to yourself.

_____

_____

_____

_____

_____

_____

_____

_____

_____

_____

_____

_____

_____

_____

With the arrival of Jesus, the Messiah, that fateful dilemma is resolved. Those who enter into Christ's being-here-for-us no longer have to live under a continuous, low lying black cloud. A new power is in operation. The Spirit of life in Christ, like a strong wind, has magnificently cleared the air, freeing you from a fated lifetime of brutal tyranny at the hands of sin and death.

Romans 8:1

The Message Bible

I AM FORGIVEN....

*M*uch is spoken to the victims of infidelity to inspire their healing. The spouse that is left behind to pick up the pieces most times will receive all the attention and support needed to start life over again. Yet, while they are rebuilding their lives and learning how to trust love again, the spouse who cheated is left alone to count their regrets. Who notices the downward spiral of the spouse left to bear the burden of self-resentment and condemnation?

When you decide to break a covenant in a relationship, something is already broken and hurting on the inside of you. There is usually a void going unfulfilled – a void that your current spouse could not fill. Most likely, you entered the marriage, expecting to find completion. After the "I Do's," when you found yourself still lonely or unhappy, disappointing as it may be, you continued to seek to have the void filled. You were pursing wholeness, even if that meant going outside of your marriage to find it.

Your void may have been the result of the death or abandonment of a parent. Maybe your void came as a result of some type of childhood abuse and trauma. After being abandoned as a child, you may have possibly navigated countless relationships looking for a place to fit in. Through years of broken relationships, you have continued to seek that one person who would make all the painful memories dissolve.

There is healing for you too. The people who you have hurt have a right to be hurt. They have every right to be angry. Forgiveness is equally available to you also. It may take a long time for your ex to forgive you. It may take time for the children to forget the pain and helplessness they experienced as they watched you pack your things and leave. As others work to heal, there are two critical things you must do in your efforts to move forward. The first thing you must do for yourself is to acknowledge and accept responsibility for your mistakes. Immediately following that, the most important three words you will ever need to begin to tell yourself are these: *I AM FORGIVEN.*

Today's Reflection:

In yesterday's reflection, we acknowledged the errors we made that ultimately drove our relationship over a cliff. In today's reflection, let's take a deeper look inside to better understand why we made those decisions. Don't be afraid to be honest here - this is your private journal. No one has to see the words on this page except you. Even though God's promises are not nullified by our mistakes, we are still left with the work to identify where we need to grow. We must do the work. What unresolved issues from your past and/or flawed personality traits do you believe contributed to the lack in judgement on your part?

_____

_____

_____

_____

_____

_____

_____

_____

_____

_____

_____

_____

_____

_____

What do you think? With God on our side like this, how can we lose? If God didn't hesitate to put everything on the line for us, embracing our condition and exposing himself to the worst by sending His own Son, is there anything else He wouldn't gladly and freely do for us? And who would dare tangle with God by messing with one of His chosen? Who would dare even to point a finger? The One who died for us—who was raised to life for us! –is in the presence of God at this very moment sticking up for us. Do you think anyone is going to be able to drive a wedge between us and Christ's love for us? There is no way!

Romans 8:37
The Message Bible

DON'T DOUBT
YOURSELF...

*a*fter several years of hoping and praying that she would eventually marry her high school sweetheart, she finally accepted the fact that the relationship that she had kept on life support had died long ago. The young man that she fell in love with during her sophomore year was nothing like the man who he had become. Physically he looked the same, and hugging him felt the same. But loving him felt extremely different. She had broken up with him at the end of her senior year. Weirdly, after two abusive marriages, she had begun to doubt why she left him in the beginning.

After running into each other in the mall, now, here they were as adults looking for a second chance at love. He never validated the relationship. But because of their history and what he represented in her life, she never considered that this was indeed a *situationship*. Even worse, as intimate as the experience felt to her, because of her fear of losing him again - she would foolishly continue to wait at the doorstep of his heart. She waited and anticipated for several years for him to come around and make her the queen. That never happened.

She painfully realized, the same person she had grown frustrated with as a young girl, had reappeared. The same communication flaws resurfaced, and she spent many nights in tears tormented by the fear of another broken dream. She held on as long as she could—learning that it is not possible to grasp or cling to a "shadow" of love. Ultimately, she realized that her childhood sweetheart hadn't changed at all. She had. She was not the same naive and broken girl that fell in love with him all those years ago.

Being the first to say goodbye takes courage. It can be quite scary to assume the responsibility of ending a relationship. You might think, what if my spouse can change? What if our breakthrough is right around the corner? What if someone else gets to experience the change in them that I have waited so long to see? But in this space, we must learn to trust wisdom and our instincts. There you will discover that you've got the guts to do what must be done.

As you mature emotionally, the more difficult it becomes for you to cling to unhealthy relationships. No matter what the chances are for success, if it's not *right for you*—it's just not *for you*. If you have walked away from a relationship, unsure of what the future holds, applaud your courage. Don't doubt yourself—don't look back. Typically, your first decision is the right one. Now, trust your judgment and trust that your bright future is in God's hands.

Today's Reflection:

Trusting the unknown can be downright frightening! Yet, with God's help and the guidance of the Holy Spirit, we can learn how to avoid unnecessary disappointment and trauma. Sometimes we have to let go of the dreams we hold dear to receive God's best for us. What dreams have brought you hurt and pain? Is it a career path that you need to change? Is it a wayward teenager you need to release to God? Is it a business you can't seem to find success in? Maybe there is a relationship you have had on life support for far too long. In today's reflection ask God to reveal the things He wants you to release so that you can move forward. Remember, letting go doesn't mean you have failed. It just means that you have awakened to receive something better.

_____

_____

_____

_____

_____

_____

_____

_____

_____

_____

_____

_____

_____

"My grace is enough; it's all you need.

My strength comes into its own in your weakness."

Once I heard that, I was glad to let it happen. I quit focusing on the handicap and began appreciating the gift. It was a case of Christ's strength moving in my weakness. Now I take limitations in stride, and with good cheer, these limitations that cut me down to size—abuse, accidents, oppositions, bad breaks. I just let Christ take over! And so the weaker I get, the stronger I become.

2 Corinthians 12:9

The Message Bible

9

HIS GRACE IS SUFFICIENT...
NOW START WALKING!

I love baseball! There is nothing like the springtime of year when thousands pack the stadiums and little league fields and watch as young men and women, boys and girls, each pick up a bat and take a swing at a ball coming at speeds up to 95 mph. They each get three swings--three chances at being the one to hit a famous home run that will make them MVP of the game. Yet many, if not most, will either strike out or only get a base hit.

After my husband left our children and me, I realized this was my 3rd strike! This was the 3rd of three long term broken relationships. I had swung three times looking for that home run. But once again, this relationship was not built on a firm foundation. This time like the others, I was doing things my way and expecting God to bless my disobedience. Once again, I was doing the swinging and not allowing God a chance at bat. I didn't have the patience to wait for God to swing. I knew that if I put him up to plate, he would stand there forever, taking His time. Balls would come His way, and He wouldn't even take a swing. And I just couldn't wait for that, so I stepped up to plate on my own and struck out!

When we impatiently rush in our decisions on what mate to settle down with, we are silencing the inspiration and direction of God. Most times, these relationships don't turn out well. We either end up broken in divorce, or we remain in a lifeless and unhealthy relationship out of obligation. On the other hand, when we allow God to come up to the plate with us, He will guide us in our decision making. He will show us how to be patient and watch for which balls to avoid. His Holy Spirit will reveal the curve balls and the fly balls before we take a swing at them – sparing us another strike. After so many balls come my way, while I stand there patiently, not swinging at the curve balls – His grace finally releases me to walk to 1st base without even swinging. When I let God take over, the weaker I get – and the stronger I become!

On moving day, I packed my children in the car. The truck began to pull out of the driveway for the last time. I looked back and took one last look at our house filled with a combination of good memories, nightmares, and broken dreams, I looked back at the strikeout. Then, I looked up towards heaven and said, "Okay, God, you're up!"

Today's Reflection:

Have you ever struck out in love before? Have you ignored God's voice and taken a chance on romance despite the red flags? In today's reflection, reflect on that relationship and the humbling experience of letting go. There is only one good way to fail – failing forward.

_____

_____

_____

_____

_____

_____

_____

_____

_____

_____

_____

_____

_____

_____

_____

_____

_____

No temptation has overtaken you
except such as is common to man;
but God is faithful,
who will not allow you to be tempted
beyond what you are able,
but with the temptation will also make the way of escape,
that you may be able to bear it.
1 COR. 10:13
The Message Bible

10

YOU'RE IN HIS HANDS....

God sees the tears you've cried; He knows the pain you have felt inside. At times you may have wondered why He has allowed you to go through this crisis. You may wonder why He would allow you to do things your way. But God has His hands on you. He will not let you go any further than your breaking point. The Father will bend you, and He will mold you. Then, if His image in you becomes flawed, He will break you. Still, He is right there with you. He has every intention of putting you back together again.

We tend to think that when we go against God's plan for us, that He doesn't already have a resolution for the problem we have created for ourselves. We think that because we have messed up again, we are now alone in a hopeless situation. That is not so! Nothing that you are going through right now is taking God by surprise.

As you sit there with your head hung low in shame and defeat, know this: He has already provided a way of escape for you and His Holy Spirit to lead you to it. Even when you think you're off track, you may discover a purpose for that part of the experience as well. Somewhere down the road in your journey, the lesson learned from that broken relationship will be needed. You will be grateful for having had the experience.

Today is your day, release those tears and allow them to wash the pain away. Your tears are valuable for cleansing the soul. Then, trust Christ to wipe the tears away. Christ is not so far separated from us that he cannot feel our pain. He did not die for us without knowing the severity of our emotions. He understands precisely how we feel. He is not ignorant of the *dis*-eases of our hearts. When Christ died, he died so that we may have access to authentic and everlasting healing. By His stripes, you are healed. By His stripes, you are redeemed. Furthermore, because he was wounded, you are free to be free!!

Nothing you nor I could ever do will separate us from His protection. Just think about it! Here you are still standing after divorce. Still standing after abuse. Still standing after being abandoned and left for dead. If you didn't know by now, You're in His hands.

Today's Reflection:

It's time to make a firm decision to live each day knowing that you are not in this alone. It's time to resolve to forgive ourselves and others for the disappointments in the past. Whether they have apologized or not, it's time to move forward with the grace God gave us. When we let go and give our broken hearts to God, then He can heal us. His affirmation gives us the strength to arise and move forward. In today's reflection, describe how your perspective on failed relationships have evolved over the last 10 days.

_____

_____

_____

_____

_____

_____

_____

_____

_____

_____

_____

_____

_____

_____

PART II.

THIRSTING FOR HIM

A white-tailed deer drinks
from the creek;
I want to drink God,
deep draughts of God.
I'm thirsty for God-alive.
I wonder, "Will I ever make it—
arrive and drink in God's presence?"
I'm on a diet of tears—
tears for breakfast, tears for supper.
All day long
people knock at my door,
Pestering,
"Where is this God of yours?"
Psalm 42:1-3 The MSG

A PRAYER FOR GOD'S SUSTENANCE

*F*ather, I am thirsty for You. All this time, I thought relationships would quench my thirsty soul. I thought that money would bring me peace in the absence of a mate. I thought accomplishments, rewards, and acclamations would sustain me. But, none of these have kept their end of the bargain. None of these are there at night in the silence when I am crying out for embrace. None of these are there when I find myself confused and all alone. God, I am left to conclude that only You can fill this empty void in me. I need Your unfailing love; not just a representative of love, or a counterfeit. I don't need sex, nor do I need the affirmation of my physical appearance from others. I don't need someone hanging around in my life because of what they think they can get from me. But I need Your authentic, soul-deep love. I want to know the love that will allow me to forgive those who have hurt me. I want to know what it feels like to love and be loved beyond my deficiencies. I want to know the genuine love that looks beyond my flaws and imperfections and sees me as whole. I need love that looks beneath the surface and can touch my hidden wounds; hidden wounds like fear, distrust, and insecurity. My broken heart has been bruised and scarred by those who lied about love. Others have used the sacrilege of love to rob me of what *they* lacked. Now, I need to feel You. I have come a long way on this journey and I can't go back the way I came. To move forward, I need to know You in a much deeper way. I desire to know how is it that You can look at me, observe my disobedience and still love me? You continue to come alongside me, help me to pick up the pieces and clean up my messes, wiping the slate of my sins clean as a whistle. That's the love I need to know. My heart is open to You, so I can worship You in spirit – and in truth. Now, pour in as much of your love as I can take. I need Your love Father. Without it, I am nothing. *Amen.*

"This is how much God loved the world: He gave His Son, His one and only Son. And this is why: so that no one need be destroyed; by believing in him, anyone can have a whole and lasting life. God didn't go to all the trouble of sending his Son merely to point an accusing finger, telling the world how bad it was. He came to help, to put the world right again.

John 3:16-18

The Message Bible

FOR GOD SO LOVED...

or God so loved the world that *He gave*. Many people associate love with a touch or a feeling you have about someone with which you are experiencing a physical and mental attraction. However, intimacy should not be reduced to something so insignificant. The first expression of love we should refer to is the love that compels us to give. I'm not relating to the material gifts of love. I'm not referring to jewelry, a new home, or a pocket watch here. Yet, I am pointing to the invisible, yet tangible gifts of love.

When I hear someone say I love you or I'm so in love with him/her, I first wonder what did you give? When you consider giving as an essential aspect of loving, then the authenticity of love becomes evident. Millions of marriages have ended in divorce simply because of the misconception that if I give them the world, then they will love me. That's not the truth. Let's take a look at what God gave. First, He gave something no one else could provide - *redemption*. Secondly, God gave the one thing that meant the most to Him, *His spirit*. Lastly, He gave something that could not be replaced, *Himself*.

The word 'love' is generally used in verb form suggesting an action to be performed. What did God *do*? He loved! Furthermore, how did he demonstrate his love? He loved so strongly that He had to *give*. It would be fitting to say here that the words *loving* and *giving* are synonymous.

Answer this, how can you be loving if you are not making an offering? Are you genuinely giving if you are not giving from a heart that loves? True love, God's love, knows no limits. Therefore, when we love, we should be compelled to give. And in our delivery, our giving should know no boundaries.

Today's Reflection:

If you are not giving, then you are not loving. In todays' reflection, think about your level of giving in relationships. Are you a giver or a taker? Do you give freely, or do your gifts come with conditions? Are you more prone to give your money, your time, or your body? How often you give in acts of service? What aspect of giving have you identified that you need to grow in?

_____

_____

_____

_____

_____

_____

_____

_____

_____

_____

_____

_____

_____

_____

_____

I am absolutely convinced that nothing – nothing living or dead, angelic or demonic, today or tomorrow, high or low, thinkable or unthinkable—absolutely nothing can get between us and God's love because of the way that Jesus our Master has embraced us.

Romans 8:38-39

The Message Bible

12

NOTHING SHALL
SEPARATE ME FROM HIS LOVE...

I can give you my journey. I can give you my heart. I can lay down my will and open my heart to receive yours. I can be there when you need a shoulder to cry. I can listen even when you can't hear your own thoughts. I can climb mountains and cross seas if it means that I will meet your love on the other side. I can forsake all secondary agendas and make you my daily motivation and priority."

So often we look for someone to say these words to us and mean them. We spend our days and nights wishing there was someone to look into our eyes and see the depths of our souls. If only we could find someone who would look beneath the skin, beyond the money, and past our title. Life would be much more meaningful if such a person would show up and calm our silent fears of loneliness. Waking up each morning would be much more delightful if the warm embrace of affirmation greeted us.

The tragedy is that many of us live and die, never having realized that God said those very words to each of us when He created heaven and earth. Then He repeated it when He gave His son Jesus Christ as a ransom for our souls. God loved us so much that He crossed heaven and earth to get to us. He gave us His journey and affirmed our very existence. He made us the apple of His eye, His top priority, and His daily motivation.

No single person on earth could ever fill the void that was intended for Him to fill. Right now, instead of longing for the perfect soulmate to satisfy your desires, look to the Father who loved us without limits. When you start looking to Him, you will find that Love was right there all along.

Today's Reflection:

Affirmation is like the foundation a house is built upon. Affirmations can be negative or positive. The good thing is that we get to choose how we affirm ourselves. Will we build ourselves up or tear ourselves down? Positive affirmations are empowering statements with the power to challenge your negative self-perception and correct a negative thought pattern. When we repeat positive affirmations regularly and apply a firm belief system to a positive outlook, our lives change almost instantly. In today's reflection, identify the most common negative self-sabotaging thoughts running rampant in your mind. List them out here. Then, right beside the negative thought, list the positive promises of God that will annul the negative idea.

NEGATIVE THOUGHTS	GOD'S PROMISE

_____

_____

_____

_____

_____

_____

_____

_____

_____

_____

There has never been the slightest doubt in my mind that the God who started this great work in you would keep at it and bring it to a flourishing finish on the very day Christ Jesus appears.

Philippians 1:6

The Message Bible

13

HE HAS BEGUN
A "GOOD WORK" IN YOU...

When you look in the mirror, do you like what you see? Do you zoom in to focus on the flaws and scars? When you look back throughout your life, do you look back with regrets as you count every mistake and wrong decision? Be reminded that before you were formed, God knew you. He knew each day, moment, and event that would take place in your life. And yet still, He saw the value in you. You were worth something to Him. So, ask yourself this, "What am I worth to me?"

The sum of your worth cannot be found by looking at your accomplishments and subtracting your failures. If you can identify with how much you mean to Him, you will then discover your weight in glory. You are not just a mistake of your parents or a wreck waiting to happen. You are a masterpiece carefully designed by the Master Creator Himself. He could not have created a better you, and He is satisfied with His work. So, there is nothing you could do to perfect His work in you. You can add whatever beauty enhancements available on Amazon or in the shopping mall. But you cannot ever exceed *His glory* in you. He decides what is beautiful!

We attend universities and pursue multiple degrees. We work harder and harder on our jobs to pursue titles that we believe add value to our names. We alter our images to keep up with society's ever-changing definition of beauty. It can be quite scary to let go of the desire to become and just simply BE. You might think, "What will others say when they see me enjoying life as it stands today?" No matter what you see when you look at your journey, find the courage to love yourself just the way you are. There is nothing you can add to or take away from your life that can create a better you, than the one He has already created. There could never be a more beautiful you than "the you" God sees today.

Today's Reflection:

There is more to you than meets the eye. You are an everlasting spring of God-energy. Your greatest value exists beneath the surface of your being. There are some treasures down on the inside of you that only you and God know about. Then there are still other treasures you possess, that you have not discovered yet. Before you complete today's reflection, may I suggest that you spend some time in silent meditation or worship? Pray and ask God to reveal the treasures you possess that you have not known before now. Then journal your discovery here.

_____

_____

_____

_____

_____

_____

_____

_____

_____

_____

_____

_____

_____

_____

_____

_____

When I was a child, I spoke as a child, I understood as a child, I thought as a child; but when I became a man, I put away childish things.

1 Corinthians 13:11

NKJV

14

PUTTING AWAY
CHILDISH THINGS...

hen I was growing up, like other children, at Christmas time, I received all sorts of toys and games that were age appropriate. Each year, I didn't notice that the things I got a year or two before had disappeared. Of course, my mother had thrown them away. The toys were either broken, or I had just outgrown them. Amazingly, it never seemed to bother me that they were missing; I was now paying attention to the new age-appropriate toys and games.

The same goes for love. With each new relationship, we are allowed to learn and grow in our ability to love. Once we have outgrown that relationship, either the relationship itself will have to transform to accompany us in our new state, or we will have to move on to the next level without them gracefully. This transition can sometimes be painful when somebody feels left behind. Most times, they just will not understand.

Sometimes, we will look up and realize that God has removed the people, things, and goals that we once held dear to us from our lives. We don't know how it happened. Somehow you just seemed to grow apart. But like my mother removing the toys while I wasn't looking, this is God's way of telling us we have outgrown these relationships. As a reward, He will replace it with another dream or relationship that is more age appropriate.

Real love will challenge our hearts to grow and mature. It causes us to put away childish things (like insecurities, self-doubt, distrust, fear, selfishness, bitterness, unforgiveness, etc.) When we mature in love, we find out that everything that we thought *was* love - *was not* love at all. We eventually discover that many of the things we thought were true about love were lies. Remember, authentic love knows no boundaries. God is Love, and He places no conditions on who He is to us. Once we discover what love *is*, we will accept what love *is not*.

Today's Reflection:

Putting away childish things means growing in our relationship with God emotionally and spiritually. When we develop a right loving relationship with Him, we cultivate the courage to avoid and release any relationship that is not aligned with His will for our lives. In today's reflection, create some time for personal worship. Just 10 minutes alone in His presence can feel like hours. Then, reflect so that you may discover the things you need to put away in pursuit of a mature relationship with Him. Journal your discoveries here.

Now that you've cleaned up your lives by following the truth, love one another as if your lives depended on it. Your new life is not like your old life. Your old birth came from mortal sperm; your new birth comes from God's living word. Just think: a life conceived by God himself! That's why the prophet said,

The old life is a grass life,

its beauty as short-lived as wildflowers;

Grass dries up, flowers droop,

God's word goes on and on forever.

This is the word that conceived the new life in you.

1 Peter 1:22

The Message Bible

15

GIVING THE GIFT
OF GOD IN YOU...

*T*he greatest gift of all is Love. It is truly the gift that keeps on giving. When we relate to one another in the form of a relationship, we will most times bump into each other's real character. Many times, what lies beneath the surface of the kindness and warm fuzzy feelings are a myriad of imperfections. As we attempt to love the person from the inside out, we will grow in our ability to accept people as they are. Hence, *loving the unlovable* begins.

It is not easy to look at someone else's flaws and say, "I love you anyway" (especially when those flaws affect us or have the capacity to harm us in some way). Jesus demonstrates in his passionate story about love, that it is possible to look beyond the veil of hurt and see them through the lens of grace. Since we do not have to endure even half the pain that he suffered - it's very likely.

In his life's journey, Jesus showed us all how to take our broken hearts to the Father and ask Him to mend the broken pieces. At the tomb of Lazarus, Mary and Martha doubted him. Judas betrayed him. His beloved Peter denied ever knowing him. Even more so, after he spent his life healing and serving them, the Jews persecuted, lied on, and crucified him. Yet, Jesus showed us the importance of sneaking away daily to spend time alone with the Father. This demonstration of worship is how he got the strength to love his enemies and forgive his loved ones. Here is where he unleashed his tears and most heartfelt concerns.

Real authentic love is not just there to fill our voids of loneliness or the need to be embraced. But genuine love should draw us to our knees to God. If love is effective, *that* love catapults us into a closer relationship with the Father.

Today's Reflection:

In our search for an expression of God's love through others, we will be introduced to each other's imperfections. When we are faced with the flaws that are not apparent to the naked eye, we are faced with two options: 1.stay and embrace them or 2. reject them and run for the hills. And that decision is evident for *both* parties. We are all flawed. In today's reflection, describe the imperfections and flaws others will discover in their intimate encounter with you.

Peter said, "I don't have a nickel to my name, but what I do have, I give you: In the name of Jesus Christ of Nazareth, walk!" He grabbed him by the right hand and pulled him up. In an instant, his feet and ankles became firm. He jumped to his feet and walked.

Acts 3:6
The Message Bible

16

BUT WHAT I DO HAVE,
I GIVE IT UNTO YOU...

God challenges us to seek His best for us. But God knows what is best. When we approach relationships as immature children, we show up looking for what we can get out of the relationship. We tend to view the other person as simply "a means to an end". Because of our selfish nature, we also tend to determine a person's love for us by their willingness to meet our demands.

As we mature to understand what authentic love is, it is crucial that we first understand what it *is not.* We must first accept that love does not seek to please itself. God is Love and was surely not aiming to please Himself. When Adam and Eve sinned in the garden, if it were not for Love, He would have destroyed them and started His work over again. But instead, God showed them His love by maturing them. He didn't immediately restore their inheritance. Instead, over many years, God blessed them with family, land, and long life. Over hundreds of centuries, He continued to demonstrate His love – even by giving His Son to redeem a broken humanity.

God displays His Love in how He cares for us – day by day. His example showed us that Love is synonymous with service. For anyone who has ever been in need, you understand that you don't have the luxury of being picky. If it is love you stand in need of, you do not have to choose. The greatest love of all is available to you. Your only challenge will be rising to receive it.

Today's Reflection:

When God does not appear to answer our prayers, we tend to place His love for us on trial. We think maybe we have done something to be disqualified from His love. Or we may start to default to the idea that He never loved us *at all*. The fact is, He *has* answered our prayer. But, the answer may not have been the one we were hoping for. This is also a demonstration of His love for us. In today's reflection think about a time when You prayed and asked God to do something – but the situation did not change in your favor. Is it possible that His love for us was demonstrated by protecting us from our own misguided desires?

_____

_____

_____

_____

_____

_____

_____

_____

_____

_____

_____

_____

_____

_____

_____

_____

"But He knows where I am and what I've done.
He can cross-examine me all He wants, and I'll pass the test
with honors.
I've followed Him closely, my feet in His footprints,
not once swerving from His way.
I've obeyed every word he's spoken,
and not just obeyed his advice—I've treasured it."

Job 23:10
The Message Bible

17

HE GUARDS THE LIVES
OF HIS FAITHFUL ONES...

*W*ho is your guard? Over the years, I can only thank God for guarding my life. It has been painful most times to have Him remove people from me. He wanted to detach me from people I desperately wanted to cling to for validation or security. Having a pure heart has often caused me to be so optimistic and forgiving to the point of bringing harm to my own life. But God, my Guard, knows what's best for me. The lust in our eyes and the passion in our hearts can quickly deceive us. So like metal detectors in an airport, God will use His spiritual light beams to expose anything that would bring us harm or take us away from Him.

But after a little time passes and as the healing process begins, I begin to thank Him for being my Guard. He has shielded my life like the British soldiers have defended the Royal Palace. He loves me so much that He stands as a guard around me watching and protecting me from intruders whose purpose is to do me harm. Prison guards typically undergo extensive training on how to recognize a threat. They are taught how to identify the threat in advance and repel any opportunity for attack. In the same manner, My Guard always has greater insight than I do. So even when I may think someone is an excellent fit for me, He in His infinite wisdom, turns them away for my greater good.

He is the Guard at the gate. He never sleeps, he never flinches, He never stops to use the restroom. He never leaves his post. He will not allow the enemy to slip past Him. Even when I am preoccupied with my itinerary and desires, He stands guard with His flashlight and detectors, inspecting those who attempt to enter my life. Everyone who wants to secure a place in my life must come through Him. Furthermore, if they are found to be carrying weapons of destruction, He abruptly turns them away. He rejects them at the gate—*access denied.*

With time spent in prayer and therapy our wounds can become healed. But we should also learn that no matter how much we love, forgive, and seek the best in a person, God loves us so much that He will even guard us against ourselves.

Today's Reflection:

Has God protected you from a dangerous relationship? Has He blocked the path so that distractions would not throw you off course? Maybe you've wanted to be accepted into a certain clique or social organization. Maybe you wanted a certain job. Your very existence is so valuable to God, that He is resilient in His efforts to protect the promises He has spoken over your life. In today's reflection, think about the times that God has kept you on the straight and narrow path towards your purpose.

_____

_____

_____

_____

_____

_____

_____

_____

_____

_____

_____

_____

_____

_____

_____

_____

"Don't fear: I am First. I am Last. I'm Alive. I died, but I came to life, and my life is now forever. See these keys in my hand? They open and lock Death's doors, they open and lock Hell's gates..."

Revelations 1:18a

The Message Bible

18

HE DELIVERS US FROM THE HANDS OF THE WICKED...

*C*orrectional officers have extremely aggressive jobs. Pacing the floors of criminals judged to be a threat to the public, they are required to show no signs of weakness. Throughout their entire shifts, they must consistently walk in authority. They must keep their eyes and ears open to always monitor every move of each prisoner. They know that one wrong step or even the smallest mistake can present a threat to themselves, the other prisoners, or the outside population.

It is also critical that prison guards perform routine cell checks, or some may call them "shakedowns." Prisoners are only allowed to have specific items necessary for their day-to-day survival in their possession. Having unapproved property in their possession would likely result in further disciplinary action. The guard has all authority to confiscate it at once.

Like a correctional officer, God will check the cells of the wicked. He will regularly go behind their bars to inspect everything in their possession. He may find riches, and he may inspect their health. In His quest, God may even discover they have stolen the shattered pieces of your heart. Anything that does not belong to them, by His authority, is confiscated - at once. That includes you. When the Lord finds that the enemy has taken you captive into his cell, God's authority will deliver you. You belong to Him! Your enemies have no power, and at the command of the Guard, you are released and set FREE!

Today's Reflection:

God will stop at nothing to retrieve you from the hands of the enemy. You were bought at a price and redeemed at an expensive cost. The enemy has no authority or rights to your heart, so when he oversteps his boundaries, God is relentless in His pursuit of you. In today's reflection, think about a time when you felt emotionally trapped and spiritually bound? How did God recover you from this state? What is it about you that God is so willing to exhaust His resources in pursuit of you?

_____

_____

_____

_____

_____

_____

_____

_____

_____

_____

_____

_____

_____

_____

_____

_____

The blessing of ADONAI is what makes people rich,
and He doesn't mix sorrow with it.

Proverbs 10:22

Complete Jewish Bible

19

HIS BLESSINGS
DON'T BRING SORROW...

*A*ll our relationships begin with a period of euphoria, often called the honeymoon phase. During this period, we are mostly in love with the idea of being in love. Everything the other person does is lovely. We only see the good, and we are blind to the bad. Warning signs and red flags are going off all over the place. Sadly, we choose to ignore them because this person makes us feel amazing.

Then, eventually, the euphoria fades, and the work it takes to keep the relationship going becomes a chore. The real character of our lover is exposed. And though they are telling us who they are with their actions, we just refuse to believe them. Sadly, most times, one person in the relationship will continue to hold on to the memories of the honeymoon; while the other side has already packed their bags, checked out, and turned in their keys. Though the neglect and feelings of abandonment worsen, they refuse to wake up from the dream. Days, weeks, and months may go by without any reciprocation of love. The side that holds on willingly suffers in sorrow with high hopes of the return of their loved one.

God's blessings should always add joy to our lives. His blessings are never intended to bring us sorrow. Sorrow is deep distress, sadness, or regret, especially for the loss of someone or something loved. If someone loves us the way God does, then that love should not cause us to suffer. This does not suggest that healthy relationships will not come with hardships. Yet, those hardships come with the grace to endure the challenges presented without deep sorrow.

Think about it. God's love never causes us to suffer. Therefore, the relationships He intends for us to encounter are those that give us beauty for ashes and joy for mourning.

Today's Reflection:

When God blesses us, it is to invite us into an abundant balanced life. It is His desire that we are healthy and whole inside and out. It is His desire that the framework of our families is affirmed with His love and genuine admiration towards Him and one another. We must be careful to examine what may appear to be a blessing before inviting it into our homes and families. In today's reflection, take inventory. What rewards might you have accepted into your lives that have only resulted in some form of hurt, shame, pain, chaos, or trauma?

It wasn't so long ago that you were mired in that old stagnant life of sin. You let
the world, which doesn't know the first thing about living, tell you how to live.
You filled your lungs with polluted unbelief and then exhaled disobedience. We
all did it, all of us doing what we felt like doing, when we felt like doing it, all of
us in the same boat. It's a wonder God didn't lose his temper and do away with
the whole lot of us. Instead, immense in mercy and with an incredible love, he
embraced us. He took our sin-dead lives and made us alive in Christ. He did all
this on His own, with no help from us! Then He picked us up and set us down in
highest heaven in company with Jesus, our Messiah.

Ephesians 2:4-5

The Message Bible

20

UNFORSAKEN LOVE...

There is no relationship and no sin that can keep us off God's radar. No matter how far we think we have gotten away from His presence, He is still there with us. Sometimes it should cause us to wonder though, have we abused His love? We have each experienced, at one time or another, the emptiness of a broken heart. We then think that Love has left us, or that we never had it at all.

When we are on the quest to find God's love on earth, we often get tangled up in everything else but love. We get tangled up in lust, codependency, fear of loneliness, etc. Even though we label these things love, for as long as we can, eventually, God will reveal Himself and reveal to you that what you are experiencing is *not* His love. He will demonstrate His love to you and then say, "Okay, now compare *that* to My love." Now, unfortunately, we are forced to accept the harsh reality that the person who we thought loved us only used us to fill their empty tanks. The minute we fail or disappoint them, in their book, we are no longer worthy of their version of love.

God loves us so much that even in our sin, even in our mistakes and inadequacies – He will never discard us. We belong to Him. He says, "You are mine. I don't care that you traded me for a superficial love experience. I love you enough to deliver you from your mistakes." God says, "I know you are seeking real love. I know your heart is broken. Despite everything that you have gone through, and despite the mess you think you made—I will never leave you, nor put you aside for others; I love you!"

Today's Reflection:

In today's reflection let's look at how we have grown in the last 10 days. In what ways can we begin to demonstrate our gratitude for God's resilience towards us?

_____

_____

_____

_____

_____

_____

_____

_____

_____

_____

_____

_____

_____

_____

_____

_____

_____

_____

PART III.

BETTER THAN LIFE

Because your love is better than life,
my lips will glorify you.
Psalm 63:3 NIV

So here I am in the place of worship, eyes open,
drinking in Your strength and glory.
In your generous love I am really living at last!
My lips brim praises like fountains.
I bless you every time I take a breath;
My arms wave like banners of praise to You.
Psalm 63:3 The MSG

A PRAYER OF ADORATION

*F*ather, my relationship with You, supersedes every other experience. Nothing in all Your creation has given me this level of peace. The peace that comes from knowing I am never alone—gives me strength. The joy that comes from knowing there is nothing I could ever do to lose You—gives me life. Your unfailing affection towards me propels me forward despite the rejection. Your embrace always appears when I need it most, even in times when I did not realize I needed it. While encompassed by the security of your promises, I can face life. Your shield gives me confidence when I have no other reason to believe again. In this world of weddings, careers, graduations, and material dreams – it is easy to be fooled into believing that the things I've accomplished could actually replace my relationship with You. But in reality, no relationship on Earth could hold a flame to a single moment in Your presence. No heartbreak or disappointment could reduce the value of what You have to offer. Nothing compares to You. The way you smooth out the jagged edges of my heart is amazing. You've restored my ability to smile again. I have the capacity to think loving thoughts about others, even those who are incapable of receiving Your love. I can pray for their healing and love them deeply, even if I must do it from a distance. I can keep giving the best of me to the lost, even when I'm hurting. People say about me, "Somehow you just find the strength to keep going". But *I know* that it is not me – it is You! It is always You replacing my broken cup with a new one and filling it 'til I am overflowing. No matter what I think I've lost, You always make sure that the well inside me is replenished. Father, I could go on and on about how Your love makes life worth living. But to put it simply, *Your* love is better than life. Amen!

Beloved, I pray that in every way you may succeed and prosper and be in good health [physically], just as [I know] your soul prospers [spiritually]

3 John 2

AMPC

21

NOTHING GOOD WILL BE WITHHELD FROM US....

I have had my share of heartache. Either someone has left, or either God has just dissolved a relationship because it was not His will. Still, no matter how often I go through it, it always hurts just the same. Sometimes the pain appears to worsen. When we are stripped of something or someone we hold near and dear to our hearts, it can feel like our heart has been shattered. Depending on the level of intimacy we have experienced, the grieving process can be just as dangerous as if somebody has actually died.

There is one fact though that will surely bring us back into fellowship. God promised us that He would withhold no good thing from us. We don't have a Father that would take pleasure in hiding those things that add value to our lives from us. He would never torment us by placing love out of our reach. He will not withhold anything that will bring health, peace, joy, and pleasure from us. On the other hand, it is surely His pleasure to see us living and thriving. He desires to see us prospering and in good health—even as our souls are prospering. He desires to see us whole.

Since He wants so much good for us, by any means necessary He will definitely protect us from harm. He can see the traps and storms up ahead. He can see the problems you will face down the line. For our sake, if we will heed His voice, He will intervene on our behalf. Since He is the author of our life stories, He has the power to rewrite the script. He will change the course of the story even if that means canceling your engagement. For our sake, He will save us from ourselves.

<u>Today's Reflection:</u>

Sometimes it may be difficult to decipher what God deems as "good" for us, especially when we have the culture as our guide. What appears good to man's eyes, are nowhere near what God has in store for us. Nothing this world has to offer can be compared to the love and affection that comes from God. In today's reflection, think about the superficial things this world would suggest we use to satisfy our souls. List them here. Then, in comparison, reflect on all the intangible and intrinsic rewards God offers that bring us the ultimate satisfaction.

_____

_____

_____

_____

_____

_____

_____

_____

_____

_____

_____

_____

_____

_____

"Like an open book, You watched me grow from conception to birth;
all the stages of my life were spread out before You,
The days of my life all prepared
before I'd even lived one day."

Psalm 139: 13-16
The Message Bible

22

GOD HAS A PLAN!

et back up again!" they tell me. My heart has been broken. My dreams have shattered in the blink of an eye. Still, here they are telling me to jump back up and start life again. Most times, people mean well when they attempt to encourage us by challenging us back out to the battlefield. Often times people forget that after a bad breakup or the loss of a loved one, it's important to notice that what my hurting soul needs first, is a reason to believe and hope again.

Through each test and trial, two promises remind me that it's not over. First, all things that I go through "will work together for good to them that love God." (Rom 8:28) No matter what happened - no matter who left - no matter who betrayed me - despite how I was misunderstood; He has a plan to use it. God will make sure that each of the events that led up to the tragedy (including my own missteps), will all work together to create a good outcome for me and glory for Himself. He will not allow my heart to be broken in vain. My heart may hurting today. But the tears of today, somehow, will be what causes me to sing and dance with gladness tomorrow.

Second, God has a plan! (Jer.29:11) He has meticulously planned for both the sunshine and the rain in my life. Nothing is a surprise to Him. When things look weird and just don't make sense to me, He reminds me that *He has a plan*! He has a plan to prosper me. He has planned for my hope and for a great future. He has a plan for good and not for evil. So, despite the traps my enemies may have set for me to stumble, or the unexpected losses I may experience— God's plan will prevail!

I am inspired as I remember that God has thought so *deeply* about how my story will end. He has already determined that in the end I win. We are welcomed to devise a great plan of our own and submit it to Him. But if our plan does not match His, He will cause a train wreck to stop it. My Heavenly Father has considered my ways and knows the path I should take.

Today's Reflection:

What are your plans for love? Do you plan to remain single and isolated-protecting yourself from future harm? Or do you prefer single and satisfied? Maybe your plan is remarrying again or attempt to have another child? If your business is failing, are you planning to call it quits? In today's reflection, take a moment and write out your vision. Then, when you are done, find time to pray and present your plan to the Lord. In due time, He will reveal His plan to you. Don't be surprised if His plan turns out to be greater than you could have imagined!

_____

_____

_____

_____

_____

_____

_____

_____

_____

_____

_____

_____

_____

_____

_____

_____

Late that day he said to them, "Let's go across to the other side." They took him in the boat as he was. Other boats came along. A huge storm came up. Waves poured into the boat, threatening to sink it. And Jesus was in the stern, head on a pillow, sleeping! They roused him, saying, "Teacher, is it nothing to you that we're going down?"

Awake now, he told the wind to pipe down and said to the sea, "Quiet! Settle down!" The wind ran out of breath; the sea became smooth as glass. Jesus reprimanded the disciples: "Why are you such cowards? Don't you have any faith at all?"

Mark 4:35-40

The Message Bible

23

DREAMING IN A STORM...

*L*ate one night the disciples and Jesus were out on the sea when suddenly a storm arose. They were on their way somewhere to do great ministry work, when the boat began to rock. And after doing all they could to keep the boat from capsizing, they turned to look for Jesus, finding him *fast asleep*. Being *fast asleep* suggests to us that he had fallen into a deep sleep. Imagine that! Even in the midst of a storm, Jesus found a way to block out all the noise of thunder and fall into a deep sleep.

When we decide to go to bed for the night we encounter various levels of sleep. And it takes us a while to get deep enough for our minds to create a dream. If we are at peace when we lay down to rest, sometimes, we can get to that level much faster. If we are tired and stressed out it can take longer. When life is going easy and things are going well, it's easy to build dreams. You do not have the noise of thunder, and you are not distracted by the lightning strikes. When life is good, we believe anything is possible.

But in the middle of a storm, when all hell is breaking loose in your life, your ability to dream becomes almost impossible. I've dreamed of wedding bells and fairytale endings. I've also had my dreams broken so abruptly that I didn't see the point in opening my eyes to see the light of day. When a relationship fails to give us the happily ever after we were expecting, it's difficult to find something new to believe in. Our hearts are attached to our dreams. So, when the dream is broken, our hearts want to die with them.

It was Jesus' faith that gave him the ability to fall fast asleep while in a storm. Therefore, it must be that same faith that brings us to a place of rest and contentment. The lighting may strike, and the thunder may roll. You may feel you are on the boat alone, being tossed and driven by the wind and the waves. This time take a note from Jesus: speak to your storm, fall *fast asleep*, and keep dreaming.

Today's Reflection:

In today's reflection paint the picture of your perfect storm. As you count the details of your storm, also describe how you are reacting to the storm. While everything appears to be falling apart, what are you doing? Are you pacing the floor in fear? Or are you making plans for your certain victory? The only force greater than fear is HOPE.

_____

_____

_____

_____

_____

_____

_____

_____

_____

_____

_____

_____

_____

_____

_____

_____

Just then a woman of the village, the town harlot, having learned that Jesus was a guest in the home of the Pharisee, came with a bottle of very expensive perfume and stood at his feet, weeping, raining tears on his feet. Letting down her hair, she dried his feet, kissed them, and anointed them with the perfume.

Luke 7: 36-39
The Message Bible

24

PEACE IN OUR TEARS...

*J*esus wept. This is the shortest scripture in the bible—but also the most heartfelt one in my opinion. These two words reveal the tenderness and frailty of humanity. Jesus demonstrates for us in his transparency, that no matter how strong we think we are or how close we are to God, none of us are exempt from the physical effects of a broken heart.

Like aloe treats a tear in our flesh, crying is the refreshing water that treats the wounds in our hearts. When our hearts are broken, it is natural and necessary for our bodies to produce tears. By doing so, it causes our hearts to empty itself of the bitterness and pity that would otherwise cause our hearts to become calloused. Despite the reasons why the relationship may have ended or how the pain was inflicted, our soul wants to protect our heart from future hurt. So, our soul makes a promise to our heart. It promises to build a wall so thick; no one could ever enter and do this type of damage again. Our desire for self-preservation is normal. But our tears have the power to tear the walls down and hold us open for *Him* to enter.

It is okay to cry. This is nothing to be ashamed of. It does not make us weak. The mere fact that we can cry, is evidence that God has given us His gift of love and compassion for people. We are not stones or statues without remorse. He has blessed us with the ability to *feel*. And that is what makes us strong. Our tears mean that He has given us an experience to know love and an opportunity feel His love in a tangible manner. Jesus was God wrapped in flesh. His name is *Immanuel*, which means, "God with us." As you cry take solace in the fact that God is alive *with us*. And our tears mean that He is alive *in us*. Thank God for your tears.

Today's Reflection:

When was the last time you had a good cry? In today's reflection, I want to present two options for you.

1. Close the book and find a quiet space to release the tears you may be holding in. You may want to turn on your favorite worship song and sit in meditation for a few moments first. Reflect on your life and try to recall the events that have caused you to feel hurt, pain, and shame. Acknowledge and embrace the feelings that come along with meditating on these events. As you acknowledge your feelings, and give yourself permission to grieve, call out to God in prayer and release your pain to Him. As you end this moment of release, pour out your love and gratitude for the God who catches every one of your tears.

2. Your second option is to journal and describe the last time you experienced a release like this.

_____

_____

_____

_____

_____

_____

_____

_____

_____

_____

_____

_____

The religion scholar said, "A wonderful answer, Teacher! So lucid and accurate—that God is one and there is no other. And loving him with all passion and intelligence and energy, and loving others as well as you love yourself. Why, that's better than all offerings and sacrifices put together!"

Mark 12:33

The Message Bible

25

A SWEET REUNION...

When someone manages to touch our hearts, they have entered a space rarely visited by most others. We have friends and family members who we love and admire greatly. Then when our hearts become intertwined with one another, there is a bond developed that might be devastating if broken. Only in this type of love do we begin to experience God's love on earth. The only way we will experience authentic love is through His people. When this happens, our hearts feel complete. The bible tells us to "love our neighbor as we love ourselves." (Gal 5:14) When we are courageous enough to do this, we discover that by doing so we have become one with each other and with God himself –at the same time.

To tap into love is to tap into God. There is a wholeness that comes over us that words cannot express. But as we tap in, we sometimes make the mistake of placing more focus on the person and by doing so we lose sight of the real Lover Himself. We don't necessarily fall out of love with God. Yet our human lovers sometimes steal the show. When our hearts and minds tune in to the tangible aspects of love—we get caught up in the things they do for us and how they make us feel. This can become a threat to our relationship with the Father. If God separates you from your loved one, you might be deceived into thinking that Love has left you—never to return.

God is the sole proprietary owner of your heart. He created it, therefore it belongs to Him. If He created it, then trust that He knows the pain you feel like no one else can. When your heart is broken, He knows just how to mend it. You on the other hand should always remember that it's *His* love that your soul desires. We are all vessels transporting God's love as precious cargo within us. Throughout time and beyond eternity, you have His love inside of you. Your heart may be aching as the tears continue to fall. Still, your season of heartbreak is the best time for you to fall in love with Him all over again.

Today's Reflection:

The love of God within us is resilient. This means that no matter how disappointed or broken we become, God's heartbeat never loses its strength inside us. It means that even when our loved ones leave us, the energy of love cultivated between us never dies. That energy simply lives on - *inside* of us. In today's reflection, describe a relationship that you have had to release. If it was a healthy form of love that you shared, then chances are, the energy that love created can still be felt when you think of them. How do you use the energy that love created?

_____

_____

_____

_____

_____

_____

_____

_____

_____

_____

_____

_____

_____

_____

In a well-furnished kitchen there are not only crystal goblets and silver platters, but waste cans and compost buckets—some containers used to serve fine meals, others to take out the garbage. Become the kind of container God can use to present any and every kind of gift to His guests for their blessing.

2 Timothy 2:21
The Message Bible

26

VESSEL OF HONOR...

*W*hen the Titanic set sail, it was revered as the ship that could not sink. The steel boat was built strong. It gained the affection and confidence of all those who would aboard. Many boarded this ship with their hopes and dreams packed and ready to be fulfilled. With hearts filled with hope, they would travel to a great land of opportunity. But history records a sinking like no other.

When we find love, we put great securities around it to keep it from ever being destroyed. We build the *relation*ship strong so that many would look upon us and say, "They are so strong. They can stand against anything." We enter relationships with the best intentions in mind. We are excited because finally we have found someone with hopes and dreams that mirror our own. This *relation*ship is going to take us where we've always dreamed of going. We've bought our tickets and we are ready to sail. So, we board the *relation*ship with promise filled hearts and bags packed with dreams. Then, we stand there perched on the dock, waving goodbye to anything and anyone who is not on the same boat with us.

On the course of our journey, we hit something in the sea that puts a hole in our *relation*ship. What we hit might have been betrayal, it might have been disappointment, it might have been abandonment. Soon enough, we discover the ship will not prove to be as solid as we thought. We must be reminded that God is the Master of the sea. All those that dare to set sail, should do so knowing that He has full authority to change the course of the wind as He chooses.

Today's Reflection:

If you were a container, what goodness would you possess on the inside, fit for God's good use? In today's reflection describe yourself as a container (like a can, a glass, a beautiful vase, etc.) After you've described the beauty and size of your container, then describe the contents you possess inside (like love, humility, kindness, mercifulness, etc.) In what ways, can God pour you out into the lives of others?

_____

_____

_____

_____

_____

_____

_____

_____

_____

_____

_____

_____

_____

_____

_____

From the end of the earth I will cry to You,
When my heart is overwhelmed;
Lead me to the rock that is higher than I.

Psalm 61:2

NKJV

COME UNTO ME...

Sometimes we wonder why our Father allows us to go through the pain we go through. No one can fully perceive just how much you have been hurt. Each day you may feel like your life is covered with darkness and gloom. Your future, which was once bright, now appears to be overshadowed by dark clouds. We barely want to get out of bed; our eyes hurt from the light of day. We once approached our days filled with hope and possibility. Now, to face the day is a constant reminder of what may never be. To muster up the energy to even leave our homes is excruciating. Then, to endure the hours of our long workdays can seem like a prison sentence. It may seem that you are holding your breath for hours. Then, you exhale in relief once you arrive back home and crawl back under the covers.

Jesus welcomes us to come unto him when we are weary and burdened with heavy hearts. (Matt.11:28) No matter what happened to get us here, he is ready to receive us. No matter who hurt us or who we might have hurt, his arms are always open to us. He's always ready to comfort and console us. Christ promises to take on the weight of our burdens; and we can trust him to do just that.

We have a Savior who has not left us, and He will never put us aside for another. When we hurt, he hurts. When we cry, He wipes our tears away. It does not matter what you did. We are just that important to Him. He loves us without restraint.

You have an open invitation to come to the King of Kings. He welcomes you to bring your tears to him. His arms are opened wide for you to come and bring your broken soul to him.

Today's Reflection:

In today's reflection, let's identify the things that block your path to coming to God with your burdens. Has shame kept you from approaching God with your tears. Have fear and doubt kept you from experiencing the restorative power of God's love? Has hopelessness convinced you that life can't possibly get any better?

_____

_____

_____

_____

_____

_____

_____

_____

_____

_____

_____

_____

_____

_____

_____

_____

_____

_____

This I recall to my mind,

Therefore I have hope.

Through the LORD's mercies we are not consumed,

Because His compassions fail not.

They are new every morning;

Great is Your faithfulness.

Lamentations 3:21-23

NKJV

28

THE EYE OF THE STORM...

he eye of the storm consists of clear skies and light winds. It is the most logical moment you will have amidst a turbulent season. Understanding why and how you got here begins to make sense and the winds of life aren't knocking you down. The *eye* is a break from the thunder and lightning. While standing in the eye, you can actually grasp the idea of a brighter day. It is in this moment, in the midst of your storm, where you can actually feel *and hear* God.

However, encircled around the eye of the storm, beholds a wall of the most severe of thunderstorms. It swirls around perpetually creating storms upon storms. There is thunder and lightning like you have never imagined. People say, "you're just going through the storm" and it turns into a cliché that frightens us of the unknown. Unfortunately, storms carry the stigma of danger and destruction. But when we get past the wall and finally enter the eye, we find that storms are not only dangerous, but they are necessary.

The storm, while dangerous, produces growth and stimulates change. There is an abundant and more peaceable way of living for you. Once you get to the eye of the storm you can hear, comprehend, and accept the truth. And of course, accepting truth is the beginning of finding Love. Conquering the storm requires that you find your way to the eye.

Today's Reflection:

Everett R. Storms, a schoolteacher in Canada, made a detailed study of promises. His twenty-seventh reading of the Bible took him a year and a half. At his completion, Storms reported a grand total of 8,810 promises (7,487 of them were promises made by God to humanity).

When we are in the thick of our darkest season and in the pit of our lowest valley, it's easy to lose sight of hope. If we just look up towards heaven (this simply means to stop and recall God's promises) we can be replenished with enough hope to make it through to the other side. Today, grab your bible, or maybe your bible app, or using your laptop just go to a search engine like Google. If you are using a search engine type these words "God's Promises". In the space below, list the scriptures & promises that bring hope back into view.

_____

_____

_____

_____

_____

_____

_____

_____

_____

_____

_____

_____

_____

A jug of sour wine was standing by. Someone put a sponge soaked with the wine on a javelin and lifted it to his mouth. After he took the wine, Jesus said, "It's done . . . complete." Bowing his head, he offered up his spirit.

John 19:30

The Message Bible

29

ALREADY OKAY ...

*E*ven though you are still in the thick of heartache and in the midst of your storm, you can stand right there in the eye - knowing that all things are working in your favor. Though you have loved with your whole heart and had it shattered into pieces, you can smile knowing that real, authentic love is *never* lost.

As we fearfully look towards each new day, we can find peace in knowing that our God has already conquered everything in that day. Every battle you will face already has a determined outcome. The obstacles you will encounter, God has already removed them from your path. Every conflict already has a resolution. The tears you may be scheduled to cry at lunchtime, God is prepared to wipe them away.

What we all need is the peace of knowing in our hearts that everything is *already okay.* Finding that peace may appear difficult – but getting to the eye of the storm is all we need to do. Your heart may have been broken by a failed relationship or a recent job loss. Even empty nesting after raising your children can bring deep sadness. Your plans may have been in vain, and your dreams may have been destroyed, but you are still standing. If things are chaotic and uncertain around you, pause for a moment. In your stillness, you can hear His voice of assurance calling from within. "It's already ok."

Today's Reflection:

When I am amid the storm, one of my favorite old gospel hymns is "It is well with my soul" written by Haratio Spafford. The lyrics in this song go on to say:

"Though Satan should buffet,
though trials should come,
Let this Blest assurance control.
That Christ has regarded my helpless estate,
And has shed His own blood for my soul,
It is well, It is Well, It is well with my soul."

In today's reflection describe how Christ's sacrifice gives you the strength to move forward despite the trauma and disappointment you have experienced. Feel free to rewrite your own verse to add to this old hymnal.

_____

_____

_____

_____

_____

_____

_____

_____

_____

_____

_____

_____

"I have seen his ways, but I will heal him; I will lead him and restore comfort to him and to his mourners, Creating the praise of the lips. Peace, peace to Him who is far and to him who is near," Says the Lord, "and I will heal him."

Isaiah 57:19

NKVJ

30

I WANT A PEACE...

$\mathcal{I}$ want "a peace" that escapes my ability to understand from whence it came. I want *a peace* that allows me to look my enemies in the face and smile, knowing that all is well in the end. I want *a peace* that helps me to remain calm even though it appears that all is lost. I want *a peace* that comforts my heart when I think of those who have gone on to glory and are happily in the presence of the Lord. I want *a peace* that eases the confusion in my mind, as I remember those who have used, abused, cheated on, betrayed, abandoned, and rejected me. I want *a peace* that quiets my soul when I wonder in confusion if my Lord is pleased with my living.

Many people will agree that when things have gone wrong in their lives, peace is all they really want. We can endure rejection and mistreatment and we can swallow the lump of pain lodged in our throats - if only we could find *a peace*. Some would make it sound as if peace were only an illusion; something they are grasping at in the wind.

But peace is real, and it is attainable. God has freely made it available to us. We don't have to fret or worry about tomorrow, for we will never see it. Why? Because by the time we see tomorrow it will be today. Neither does it benefit us to rehearse the failures of yesterday, because we cannot re-enter those moments in time. The key to finding peace is to let go of yesterday and cease from longing for tomorrow. We can never be at peace if our hearts are constantly torn back and forth between yesterday and tomorrow. Doing so, we are merely resisting the reality of today. We can only have *a peace* when we embrace where we are today.

Today's Reflection:

The pursuit of peace must be intentional. It can only be experienced in the current moment. In today's reflection, pause for a moment to think about your past regrets and hurts – the ones that still linger in your mind today. What are the painful memories that always seem to resurface and drive you to anger or tears when you least expect it? Then, imagine your fears and anxieties about the future. What are you most worried about?

Now, once you have them both written down, all you are left with is this present moment. Describe what works perfectly fine today? What things are going well right now? List the blessings staring back at you right now – as many as you can see.

PAINFUL MEMORIES	FUTURE FEARS	WHAT WORKS TODAY?

PART IV.

SATISFIED SOUL

hungry and thirsty,
their soul fainted within them.
Then they cried to the Lord in their trouble,
and he delivered them from their distress.
He led them by a straight way
till they reached a city to dwell in.
Let them thank the Lord for his steadfast love,
for his wondrous works to the children of man!
For he satisfies the longing soul,
and the hungry soul he fills with good things.
Psalm 107:5-9 ESV

Some of you wandered for years in the desert,
looking but not finding a good place to live,
Half-starved and parched with thirst,
staggering and stumbling, on the brink of exhaustion.
Then, in your desperate condition, you called out to GOD.
He got you out in the nick of time;
He put your feet on a wonderful road
that took you straight to a good place to live.
So thank GOD for his marvelous love,
for his miracle mercy to the children he loves.
He poured great draughts of water down parched throats;
the starved and hungry got plenty to eat.
Psalm 107:5-9 The MSG

A PRAYER OF SATISFACTION

ather, in Heaven, now I see. Now, I realize that all I ever needed was *You*. You were with me in the beginning, before you formed me in my mother's womb. Before You released me into creation, You and I were one. Your love was here first. Though my mother and my father may have forsaken me, leaving me alone to search for You - You came out to rescue me. I've discovered that Your unrelenting love for me did not end when I was born. You did not abandon me when I was separated from You in eternity. That love remained intact. Our connection was never severed. I was blind to it before, but now I know my connection to You is still strong. Your heartbeat is still alive in me. I have learned that when I sit still and get quiet enough, I can hear it loudly. I've been so distracted by what I thought was stolen from me all these years. I have been running in this direction and that one –searching for *a sound*. The sound of Your love has been drowned out by the noise of this world. But sitting still in Your presence, I can hear it now - loud and clear. And now the fire burns again. I am warmed and nourished by the heat from Your consuming fire. It feels so good to be back home, affirmed by Your loving embrace. It feels so good to be alone with You – one on one time with Your adoration of me. You have lifted me up from my ditch in the valley. You've welcomed my tears and used them to purify my soul. All my needs are met. All my questions are answered. All my anxieties are settled. Fear has lost its grip on me. I'm back where I began: with You, in the beauty of Your holiness. I am refined, and I am restored. I am satisfied with You. *Amen.*

Summing it all up, friends, I'd say you'll do best by filling your minds and meditating on things true, noble, reputable, authentic, compelling, gracious—the best, not the worst; the beautiful, not the ugly; things to praise, not things to curse. Put into practice what you learned from me, what you heard and saw and realized. Do that, and God, who makes everything work together, will work you into his most excellent harmonies.

Philippians 4:8

The Message Bible

31

CAN YOU ONLY IMAGINE...?

I can only imagine a life filled with hope. I can only imagine a life of love, not hindered by fear. I can only imagine waking up each day, with my mind free of the emotional baggage I have claimed from yesterday. I can only imagine a peace flowing so freely from within me that others come and run to take a sip. They would sip and then drink, being filled with the sweetness of God's goodness. I can imagine being so healed that when others look at me, they would not fathom that I had ever been hurt. I can only imagine having my heart so full of God's mercy, that my insecurities don't stand a chance when trying to overpower my destiny.

Are things so bad that you have thrown away the possibility of something good happening in your life? Yes, he might have left you, she might have lost the battle with cancer, or your child may have gone astray after years of sound teaching. But what about you? What about the goodness God intended for *you* to experience? Could you imagine just for one moment letting it all go... for the sake of your own good health?

Once you can begin to imagine yourself in a new life, a new body, and a new mind - then you are well on your way to 'becoming'. The same way you have allowed your mind to create all these false ideas of failure and defeat - the same way you have allowed the painful memories in your mind to run rampant creating fears of things that will likely never happen - you must train that same mind of yours to create just the opposite. Take a chance, you have nothing to lose! Go ahead! Give your mind permission to create beautiful ideas and amazing experiences in your mind that will give you something to work towards.

Today's Reflection:

If you could imagine a life on the other side of your pain, what would that look like? Do you believe you would be the strong person that you are today without having had the experience of disappointment, betrayal, or loss? In today's reflection try to imagine what your personality might be like if you had not had those experiences. Do you believe the experience has added any value to your life?

_____

_____

_____

_____

_____

_____

_____

_____

_____

_____

_____

_____

_____

_____

_____

_____

I'm not saying that I have this all together, that I have it made. But I am well on my way, reaching out for Christ, who has so wondrously reached out for me. Friends, don't get me wrong: By no means do I count myself an expert in all of this, but I've got my eye on the goal, where God is beckoning us onward—to Jesus. I'm off and running, and I'm not turning back.

Philippians 3:14
The Message Bible

32

LET IT GO...ALL OF IT!

She arrives at the airport ready to see the world. She has saved up enough money for years. The children have been raised. Though she raised her children in the church, still her only son deceased in a fatal car crash, one daughter in rehab, and her other independent daughter finally became partner with a successful marketing firm. To make matters worse, the husband who vowed to always be by her side abandoned her for another woman. She's got a lot to be upset about and a lot to run from.

But after landing in her new-found home, she waits anxiously for her bags at the airport. She checked them back before she boarded the plane. The limo is waiting for her outside. She can't wait to get to her new home. She has the right ticket. The numbers match her flight. But while standing for over 3 hours waiting for the conveyor belt to deliver her luggage, she cannot help but wonder if she made the right choice. Her daughters need her right now. They are still hurt by their father abandoning them. How could she move away from the only place she shared a life with her son?

After her 3-hour wait and several trips to customer service, she finally hears a voice inside that says, "Let it go...All of It!" And she knew what the voice meant. She had to forgive the abandoning husband: for leaving her, for tearing their family apart and for arguing with their son before he got behind the wheel. She had to forgive one daughter for turning to drugs and the other for leaving them all behind to chase her career. So as a sign of letting it all go she mercifully told the girl at customer service, "Since, I've paid for flight insurance, I'll just file a claim." Next, she gracefully flung through the doors to approach her awaiting limo— leaving all her bags behind.

As you begin to create the images of your new life, you may find that the faces of those who hurt you keep appearing. The effects of their actions still cause a lump in your throat like it happened just yesterday. This is a sign of unforgiveness. To freely move forward, there is something you must do: Drop your bags, forget about them, and go on. Forgive the hurts, the painful words, and the betrayals. Forgive your missteps. It may be difficult to release what happened. But you must abandon these past experiences and failed dreams from your heart. There is much more in store for you ahead, but you must make room to receive it. There are promises of God yet to be fulfilled in your life. Undoubtedly, He has already made provisions for where you are going. Where God is taking you, you won't need to pack a bag.

Today's Reflection:

Letting go takes courage and those who can find the strength will find great rewards in their release. In today's reflection, let's unpack. List the heavy burdens you have been carrying and the reasons why you believe you find it difficult to let go.

_____

_____

_____

_____

_____

_____

_____

_____

_____

_____

_____

_____

_____

_____

_____

_____

One day spent in Your house, this beautiful place of worship,
beats thousands spent on Greek island beaches.
I'd rather scrub floors in the house of my God
than be honored as a guest in the palace of sin.
All sunshine and sovereign is GOD,
generous in gifts and glory.
He doesn't scrimp with His traveling companions.
It's smooth sailing all the way with GOD-of-the-Angel-Armies.

Psalm 84:10-12
The Message Bible

33

IT'S TIME TO
FILE YOUR CLAIM...

*I*nsurance policies are merely promises made to *restore* you in the event of sudden trauma. Amazingly, many of us pay a premium on these policies to protect us across the span of our entire lives. The Bible is like an insurance policy. However, instead of paying a monthly monetary premium, God only requires that we maintain a consistent relationship with Him. The bible outlines all our policy terms and promises to restore us in the event of disaster. Sadly enough, many of us have never cashed in on the settlement. God's promises are not like the policies of our world where you pay a monthly premium your entire life, and then pray you never have to file a claim.

You have a right to be happy.
The LORD bless you, and keep you; The Lord make His face shine on you, And be gracious to you; The LORD lift up His countenance on you, And give you peace. Numbers 6:24-26 NASB
You have a right to be free.
He upholds the cause of the oppressed and gives food to the hungry. The LORD sets prisoners free, Psalm 146:7 NIV
You have a right to prosper.
The greedy stir up conflict, but those who trust in the LORD will prosper. Proverbs 28:25 NIV

You have a right to be healthy.
Large crowds followed him(Jesus), and he healed them there. Matthew
19:2 NIV (emphasis mine)
You have a right to laugh.
Go then, eat your bread in happiness and drink your wine with a cheerful
heart; for God has already approved your works. Ecclesiastes 9:7 NIV
You have a right to love.
And I am convinced that nothing can ever separate us from God's love.
Neither death nor life, neither angels nor demons, neither our fears for
today nor our worries about tomorrow--not even the powers of hell can
separate us from God's love. Romans 8:38 NLT
You have a right to stroll down the road and smell the roses.
I am come that they might have life, and that they might have *it* more
abundantly. John 10:10b KJV
You have a right to feel secure.
Keep your lives free from the love of money and be content with what
you have, because God has said, "Never will I leave you; never will I
forsake you." Hebrews 13:5 NIV
You have a right to sleep peacefully at night.
He makes me lie down in green pastures, he leads me beside quiet waters,
Psalm 23:2 NIV
You have a right to expect a bright future.
For I know the plans I have for you," says the LORD. "They are plans for
good and not for disaster, to give you a future and a hope. Jeremiah 29:11
NLT
You have a right to submit your claim!
Do not be anxious or worried about anything, but in everything [every
circumstance and situation] by prayer and petition with thanksgiving,
continue to make your [specific] requests known to God. Philippians 4:6

You have a right to present a claim to the Lord on His promises every
single day. And there is no cap or statute of limitations. It does not matter
how much time has passed; you are still entitled to receive everything
promised to you. Here is a challenge for you: submit your claim today!
Then, just watch the Lord make good on all His promises.

Today's Reflection:

Let's submit your claim. Despite your age, or circumstances in life –if you are alive and still breathing, you still have access to an experience with God. You can still experience the fullness of His love - in your relationships, in your finances, in your health, and even in your pursuit of happiness. You can still experience an abundant life – a life beyond your wildest dreams –but first, you must claim it! In today's reflection, write your declaration of the life of which you have always dreamed. That life is yours – just claim it!

_____

_____

_____

_____

_____

_____

_____

_____

_____

_____

_____

_____

_____

_____

_____

_____

_____

At that point Peter got up the nerve to ask, "Master, how many times do I forgive a brother or sister who hurts me? Seven?" Jesus replied, "Seven! Hardly. Try seventy times seven."

Matthew 18:21-22
The Message Bible

34

A DAILY DOSE
OF FORGIVENESS...

*F*orgiveness is like the cod liver oil my great grandmother poured on a tablespoon and held my cheeks firmly open to swallow. It was so bitter and had such a nasty taste that the flavor still haunts me to this day. One dose of cod liver oil and you were forever afraid to sneeze, cough, or breathe too loud. If she heard the sound of what *might be* illness creeping into our home, you were bound to see her coming around the corner with the bottle and a spoon. Run! But what my great grandmother knew was that it would keep me from getting sick. It prevented illness like colds and the flu. If your mother gave you a dose of this every single morning you were guaranteed to be well.

Like cod liver oil, forgiveness has a bitter taste. I don't care what you put on it to sweeten the flavor, it tastes just the same. I've never seen forgiveness swallowed easily. But because of the magnitude of the task, forgiveness is best taken in daily doses. No matter who offended you or how they did it, whether it was your fault or not - forgiveness is your dose to take – not theirs. When somebody wrongs you, their dose is confession. Yet, you cannot control their confessions. You can't drag them to the altar or seek vengeance for their wrongs. That burden lies between them and God. However, what you *can* control is your capacity to forgive.

If you wake up each morning with the thoughts or emotions attached to feelings of anger and resentment, this will not produce the abundant life you desire to live. That is why we must counteract those feelings with a daily dose of forgiveness. Holding on to resentments will cause your soul to become bitter. And a bitter soul leads to physical illnesses. The anecdote? A daily dose of forgiveness, like cod liver oil, keeps the body from becoming sick with illness. Unforgiveness is like a debt-collector, who calls on their debts every single day looking for repayment. But forgiveness will enable you to cancel the debt of the debtor and release you from the burden of a debt collector. I know it may seem the hurt is too huge. I know it appears forgiving and forgetting the past is impossible. Rest assured, all things are possible to them that believe. Think about it like this, each day that God allows us to wake up, He is taking His dose of forgiveness. As He forgives us our debts, then like our Father, we must forgive our debtors *every single day...*

Today's Reflection:

A daily dose of forgiveness requires a daily dose of courage. We don't naturally focus on forgiveness on a daily basis. We tend to only consider it when we experience an emotional trigger that places us back at the scene of the crime. Forgiveness cannot be mastered in such a *reactive* manner. To win the battle over unforgiveness, we must become *proactive* in our approach. In today's reflection, list the name(s) of the person(s) you still feel triggered by unforgiveness when you see them or hear their name. After listing the names. Write a letter of forgiveness to each person. You may feel free to share your letter with the person(s) or not. Remember, this reflection is about you opening your heart, not them being accountable for their actions.

_____

_____

_____

_____

_____

_____

_____

_____

_____

_____

_____

_____

_____

_____

Work at getting along with each other and with God.
Otherwise,
you'll never get so much as a glimpse of God.

Hebrews 12:14
The Message Bible

35

PEACE IN ACTION...

*I*t's time to let go. God's got so much for you to do. But the longer you hold on, and the longer you allow yourself to be held hostage to the pain of what has happened – the longer it will take for you to become free.

See, peace is a virtue. And like any other virtue, you must drop what is weighing you down and go after it; you must work to have it. You must surrender who you are and abandon what comes easy in order to have it. It is natural to hurt. It's natural to be confused. It's natural to want revenge. It's natural to want somebody to pay. Yet, we must surrender all of that.

Peace is also an action word. It's not just a noun; something to have and to hold. Peace is the act of making a perpetual chain of decisions that cultivate an atmosphere of peace. Instead of sitting and expecting it to come, you must *do* something. Peace does not happen on its own. Many times, to achieve peace you must do the very thing that you don't want to do. It may be picking up the phone to apologize. It may be writing a letter of release to your offender, or to yourself. Or, it may just be the simple act of getting up on your feet and moving on.

Today's Reflection:

What are you holding on to? Is it fear, is it doubt, or is it unforgiveness? Maybe it's apathy, anger, anxiety, or pride. These will only serve as impediments as you seek to build a new life after the loss of a loved one, after a bad break up, or broken dream. You will not discover real peace in your process as long as you cling to these vices. In today's reflection, first pray and ask God to reveal any hidden infections of your heart. This will likely not be a short time in prayer; I encourage you to sit in His presence silently for a while. Then, as He reveals them, make a conscious effort to release these obstacles to God. Journal your worship experience here.

_____

_____

_____

_____

_____

_____

_____

_____

_____

_____

_____

_____

_____

_____

"I am the Real Vine and my Father is the Farmer. He cuts off every branch of me that doesn't bear grapes. And every branch that is grape-bearing He prunes back so it will bear even more. You are already pruned back by the message I have spoken.

"Live in me. Make your home in Me just as I do in you. In the same way that a branch can't bear grapes by itself but only by being joined to the vine, you can't bear fruit unless you are joined with Me.

"I am the Vine and you are the branches. When you are joined with Me and I with you, the relation intimate and organic, the harvest is sure to be abundant. Separated you can't produce a thing."

John 15: 1-5

The Message Bible

180

36

SHEDDING FORGIVENESS...

ithout the shedding of blood there is no forgiveness."
(Hebrews 9:22) This is why it's so hard to release the debts
of others. We think it's much easier and less painful to just
hold on to the debt. When we imagine how we may have to be cut, we also
imagine the subsequent pain we must endure as a pre-requisite to letting
go. It's never fun to release the pain associated with our wounds. We'd
much rather just keep our hearts wrapped in bandages and keep it
moving.

I still encourage you to imagine that it is much more rewarding to
forgive and let someone off the hook. It's like this: the wounds beneath
our bandages are most times still moist and need to breathe. Allowing the
wound air to breathe helps to initiate the healing process. Therefore,
snatching the bandage off of our wounds looks like us saying to those who
have hurt us, "I forgive you and I am letting it go." Forgiving is the one
painful act that gives your heart a chance to heal. And, like snatching off a
bandage, it's only painful for a few seconds.

We all desire to experience a real lasting love, the kind that gives you
goose bumps and butterflies every day. But clinging to debts and regrets
requires that you remember and rehearse the hurt of yesterday. You've
got to keep reminding yourself why you are mad and angry. You cannot
be fully present "in love" if you are still carrying the debts of those who
have crossed you in your past.

Once we experience the real love of God, we provoked to deliver forgiveness. Here's how: when we find God's love, we then discover that with all of our faults, bad habits, and indiscretions that someone could still love us so deeply – without asking for anything in return! It is impossible to experience that and not be compelled to share it with others!

Jesus was our first real example of how to forgive the unforgiveable. You may have been raped, beaten, talked about, marginalized, stripped of your dignity, and left for dead. But like Christ, we will only gain access to *"life after hurt"* after we have shed the blood of forgiveness. You must let go and move forward. Your life depends on it.

<u>Today's Reflection:</u>

What are some destructive thoughts patterns you have developed as a result of unhealthy relationships and associations over the years? In today's reflection, let's complete a challenge. In the space below, courageously list all of the self-defeating thoughts you think about yourself – it doesn't matter how big or small you think the thought is. I promise, once you get the thoughts out of your head and down on paper, you will feel relieved indeed!

_____

_____

_____

_____

_____

_____

_____

_____

_____

_____

_____

_____

_____

_____

_____

_____

He heals the brokenhearted
And binds up their wounds [healing their pain and comforting their sorrow]
Psalm 147:3
Amplified Bible

37

I SURRENDER ALL —WITHHOLDING NOTHING

ather, today, I give it all to You. I give You the hurts, I give You the pain. I give You the memories. I give You the resentments. I give You the insecurities and inadequacies. These things add nothing good to my life. Instead, they only rob me of the fullness of joy You intended for me to experience in Your presence.

I recognize that when I am in your presence, I cannot cling to the things that block and hinder my open communication with you. I realize that if I desire a harmonic flow of love between you and I, my hands and my heart must remain open to receive from You.

So as long as I can get before You, my joy is complete. My body becomes relaxed, the lump in my throat dissolves, and the tension fades away. You said for me to cast all my cares upon You. So today I take You at Your word. I give it all to You. I don't have to try to work my fingers to the bone, in an attempt to work my own plan. I don't have to worry about how I will end up. Today, I choose to *believe* that You have a plan for me! *I believe* that You have great plans to prosper me; plans for good and not for evil.

Today, I give you everything that causes me to fear being alone. I have been abandoned and rejected. Yet, You said You are with me and would never leave me. Today I choose to *believe* you! I choose to *believe* that wherever I am, You are there also. I *believe* that You have love for me that is not worthy to be compared to Love from anyone else. So, I give all that hurts to you, *withholding nothing.*

Today's Reflection:

Now that you have done the work of forgiveness, canceling the debts, and letting it all go, Restoration is guaranteed! With restoration comes freedom - a life that knows no limits and no bounds. In today's reflection, journal what a life of liberty should look and feel like to you. It's time to abandon the ashes of hurt and shame. Let us run forward in freedom!!

_____

_____

_____

_____

_____

_____

_____

_____

_____

_____

_____

_____

_____

_____

_____

_____

So be content with who you are, and don't put on airs. God's strong hand is on you; He'll promote you at the right time. Live carefree before God; He is most careful with you.

Keep a cool head . Stay alert. The Devil is poised to pounce and would like nothing better than to catch you napping. Keep your guard up. You are not the only ones plunged into these hard times. It's the same with Christians all over the world. So, keep a firm grip on the faith. The suffering won't last forever. It won't be long before this generous God who has great plans for us in Christ— eternal and glorious plans they are!—will have you put together and on your feet for good. He gets the last word, He does.

1 Peter 5:6-10

The Message Bible

38

GETTING FREE & STAYING FREE

*T*he key to getting free and staying free is finding God's love. Though His love is always available to us, finding it can seemingly be a defeating task. The only map we are given depicting a clear path to God's love is the Bible. Yet not everyone reads it. Most times we start out on a path of walls, roadblocks, and detours. For every step we take in the right direction, something *or someone* happens to us that cause us to second guess our identity. Then, there are the snakes, lions, and wolves in sheep clothing. They strangle our ability to feel, abuse our bodies, or deceive our hearts into believing that they are what we need. When we are vulnerable and seek a safe place to rest they seduce us into their snares.

The friction in our relationships with one another will sometimes cause us to doubt God's love for us. We begin to compare His love to human love; which is always subject to fail us. God's love is not worthy to be compared. However, in His word He encourages us to love one another—just as He has loved us. Even though it appears hard and sometimes unfair, loving like God loves is possible.

To discover how God intended for us to *be loved*, we must first investigate how *HE* loves us. His love compels Him to move mountains

189

for us. His love will calm storms for us. His love will slay giants to set us free. Loving like God does not suggest that we will be flawless. However, it does suggest that we have encountered the love of God ourselves and are doing our best to resemble Him.

Today's Reflection:

Restoration is not just about finding freedom. Once you have penetrated your invisible barriers and burst into freedom – it is equally important that you also learn how to *stay there*. In today's reflection, journal about:

1. What barriers you have overcome to experience freedom,
2. New ways you have experienced God's love, and
3. Then think about what ways you will guard your newly discovered liberty against future restraint.

_____

_____

_____

_____

_____

_____

_____

_____

_____

_____

_____

_____

_____

_____

Kiss me—full on the mouth! Yes!

For your love is better than wine, headier than your aromatic oils.

The syllables of your name murmur like a meadow brook.

No Wonder everyone loves to say your name!

Take me away with you! Let's run off together!

An elopement with my King-Lover!

We'll celebrate, we'll sing, we'll make great music.

Yes! For your love is better than vintage wine.

Everyone loves you—of course! And why not?

Song of Solomon 1: 1-4

The Message Bible

39

OH! HOW HE
LOVES ME SO...

*E*ach time I look into His eyes, I melt. I have never felt this way about love before. I have never felt so good. I have never felt so accepted and cherished by anyone. I feel like the precious jewel that He will cover, protect, and allow no one to mishandle. He is mine, and I am His. Each time He touches my head I realize that all I need is Him. All I need is to see His face each day. All I need is to hear His voice whisper, "I love you".

I have lived a life of struggle, confusion, and turmoil; not knowing my name or my place. When I was found, I was in such a broken and hurt condition. I had relinquished the hope of ever experiencing the love I see in the eyes of others. My heart had been torn, ripped to shreds – and my innocence for life abused. The lions and snakes left me for dead. Then out of nowhere, He came along (*He timed it so perfectly*) and called me His own. With one word, one hug, a single glance in my direction – He washed away the pain, erased the tears, and cleaned out my memory bank! When I think of how much He cares for me and considers me—it takes my breath away. I am amazed at how He handles my enemies and silences my accusers. My Heavenly Father has redeemed me from a life of struggle. No longer can they look at me and say, "She will always be lost".

Finding His love has been my greatest accomplishment. All I need is Him. All I need is His touch, *every single day.* I have not felt the sting of loneliness since He wrapped His arms around me. Now, like a child, I run to those arms every single day. My skin feels radiant, my smile is stained across my face. And even if I doubt or begin to fear losing His love, He gently reminds me that I'm His and He will never let me go. My heart is pounding in my chest and my soul cries out, "Thank you Father for your Love!"

Today's Reflection:

I find it amazing just how often we get in our own way with negative self-talk. If only we paid more attention to all the wonderful attributes God sees in us. When God affirms us, He begins by identifying and highlighting areas where we are strong. In today's reflection, begin to think about some of the ways you are now being affirmed. What positive qualities have been revealed to you lately? What personal strengths have you discovered? What are some ways you have grown over the last 39 days?

_____

_____

_____

_____

_____

_____

_____

_____

_____

_____

_____

_____

_____

_____

_____

And I ask Him that with both feet planted firmly on love, You'll be able to take in with all followers of Jesus the extravagant dimensions of Christ's Love. Reach out and experience the breadth! Test its length! Plumb the depths! Rise to the heights! Live full Lives, full in the fullness of God.

Ephesians 3:17-19
The Message Bible

40

HOLDING ON
TO HIS LOVE...

*N*o more running to the market looking for love. Your soul can finally rest. Finding God's love was all you needed. You didn't need the shoes. You didn't need the car or the house. You didn't need the ring. It was Him *all along*.

Your Heavenly Father knows that your heart has been broken, neglected, and/or abused leaving you in a dire need to be reaffirmed by His love. It is understanding to waver in our belief that someone could love us so unconditionally, especially when we mistakenly try to compare His love to human love. Thankfully, our wavering is not a deterrent to His love. God is the Lover who will whisper, "I love you" several times a day. *He* is the Love that always abounds.

His relentless love is always chasing after us. Therefore, as we continue to seek and need Love we will always bump into Him. Every time we turn a corner looking for Love, like a thief in the night—God will steal our hearts away.

No matter what happens, despite what somebody promises you, despite any tricks your mind may play on you—keep a firm grasp on what you have found in this new place. Don't ever let it go. Surrender your heart to Him and hold fast to His Love. You may finally rest your tired soul from its quest for Love. This Love, unlike any other Love will never abandon you. This Love is always present.

Today's Reflection:

In today's reflection, describe how it feels to have a firm grip on a healthy love relationship with God.

_____

_____

_____

_____

_____

_____

_____

_____

_____

_____

_____

_____

_____

_____

_____

_____

_____

PART V.

HIS ALL-KNOWING LOVE

that according to the riches of his glory he may grant you to be strengthened with power through his Spirit in your inner being, so that Christ may dwell in your hearts through faith—that you, being rooted and grounded in love, may have strength to comprehend with all the saints what is the breadth and length and height and depth, and to know the love of Christ that surpasses knowledge, that you may be filled with all the fullness of God.

Ephesians 3:16-19 ESV

A PRAYER OF AWAKENING

Adonai, Father, I marvel at the works of your hands. I was custom made; hand crafted by Your design. No one, but You, could have ever convinced me that I was worth so much. But now that I know, the possibilities in front of me are endless. I fully understand that the way You created me was not by accident, but instead by custom design. This revelation has changed my entire perspective on life. It has changed the way I approach the mountains and the valleys. This *"knowing"* transforms my life experience beyond my understanding. See, I used to live with fear, from sun-up to sun-down. Fear of death, fear of rejection and abandonment, fear of isolation. I lived with the fear that everyone I loved would eventually abandon me. In my mind, love was always temporary. I lived with the lie that I did not deserve a healthy form of love. I lived with the shame of the things done to me. I lived with the unconscious belief that I had no value and therefore I would always struggle. *Knowing* how much You value me has changed all of that. No more fear. No more shame. No more doubt. Instead, I live with the joy that comes from understanding that I was never alone, and I never will be. I live now understanding that people will pass through my life looking for a glimpse of You, everyone is not meant to stay. So, I do not have to cling for fear of being alone. I wake up each day expecting Your presence to greet me. I now arise each day excited at the opportunity to reveal the light of Your love in all my encounters with people. I enjoy my existence, *knowing* that I was created for an especially important assignment, and You have already seen the finished work. That alone ignites me to press forward in my journey with passion. I'm enjoying my existence in spite of the odds stacked against me, in spite of those who seek my demise, in spite of the wrongs done against me – because now I know without a doubt that You have already destined me to WIN. Each day I take a moment to look towards the heavens, and I discover You smiling down on me. Father, I've been awakened to your resilient pursuit of me. My body, my heart, my soul – are all more than satisfied by your warm embrace. Now that I am awakened and alive in You, I am eternally grateful. *Amen.*

But you are a chosen race, a royal priesthood, a consecrated nation,
a [special] people for God's own possession, so that you may proclaim the
excellencies [the wonderful deeds and virtues and perfections] of Him who
called you out of darkness into His marvelous light.

1 Peter 2:9
The Amplified Bible

41

DO YOU KNOW...?

*D*o you know that self-love is different from being self-centered? It is recognizing that the invaluable glory of God *in us* radiates *through us* is to impact lives. There is something splendid about you that you may not have recognized. Now is the time to find out where your value lies. It is time to fall in love with you.

Where did you get the idea that you were unlovable? It is when we lack self-love and self-assurance that we fall into the empty traps of others. We think that if someone with more money, more status, or more education chooses to be with us, then that will validate us or increase our self-worth. We think that people will see us different. This is so *not true*! You do not want some temporary, superficial validation granted because of who you are with. You want people to notice the love, greatness, and passion for life that permeates every room you walk into!

God trusted us with something worth more than diamonds and rubies, or awards and recognition. He gave us something that cannot be compared to. He gave us something He gave to no other creation on Earth. Even before He gave us His son, He gave us something much more valuable. Himself! He gave us His image! He created us and formed us with one sole purpose: to look just like Him. We are to emanate everything that He is. Just think –we have the right and the ability to walk around with our heads held high and proudly act like, look like, and talk like him. We can think like him, and even create like him. He gave it all!

No, we are not God, but when we get into His presence, He shares His thoughts with us. His thoughts become our thoughts. Every lie the enemy has spoken about us is revealed. We begin to know the truth about who we are and what great power we possess inside. No, we are not God, but when we remain in His presence, He anoints us with the ability to create what He shows us.

When you discover all that *He is*, you begin to discover all that *you are*. Since His purpose was to create a reflection of Himself, you are His BEST work. Hence, you will begin to actually fall in love with you. Yes, you *are* all that! And for the person that left you, hurt you, and told you that you were not—they lied! In the future, now that you know what you are worth, be very selective of who you trust with your heart. Be the lifeguard who sits at the deep end of your heart. Not just anyone can dive in.

Today's Reflection:

Now that we have experienced God's affirmation, we can begin cultivating self-affirmation. Self-affirmation should not be confused with *pride*. Instead, it is the act of declaring God's word over ourselves daily. In today's reflection, read 1 Corinthians 15:10 below and journal what is revealed to you in the scripture.

But by the grace of God I am what I am, and His grace to me was not in vain. No, I worked harder than all of them -yet not I, but the grace of God that was with me.
(1 Corinthians 15:10 - Berean Study Bible)

_____

_____

_____

_____

_____

_____

_____

_____

_____

_____

_____

_____

_____

Oh yes, you shaped me first inside, then out;
you formed me in my mother's womb.
I thank you, High God—you're breathtaking!
Body and soul, I am marvelously made!
I worship in adoration—what a creation!
You know me inside and out,
you know every bone in my body;
You know exactly how I was made, bit by bit,
how I was sculpted from nothing into something.
Like an open book, you watched me grow from conception to birth;
all the stages of my life were spread out before you,
The days of my life all prepared
before I'd even lived one day.
Psalm 139:13-15
The Message Bible

ABUSED NO MORE...

After experiencing years of abuse, I am convinced that we are responsible for how others treat us. Unfortunately, we come to the tragic conclusion that the abusive relationships we find ourselves in are the best we can do. We believe the lie that that we do not deserve better.

I am not suggesting that abuse is any fault of our own. Abusers are responsible for their terrorizing behavior against those they abuse. Yet, if we are to ever break the cycles of abuse in our lives, we must hold ourselves accountable for the people we allow access to us. It is our personal responsibility to break free from abuse and begin to require the healthy love demonstrated by God from anyone we are in relationship with. Somebody will need to see a demonstration of love from you one day. But you will not have it to give if you are living a life of abuse and mistreatment.

Abuse presents itself in many forms. Emotional abuse may present itself in relationships with family members. Physical abuse may present itself at the hand of your spouse. Financial abuse may present itself in your relationship with your children. Social abuse often presents itself in your relationships with lifelong friends. However, if you study the trend, you should notice that abuse and betrayal will always come from within your closest circle of influence. People cannot hurt you or affect you unless they are in close proximity to you.

So, as you meet new people, it would be wise to measure them using God's ruler. If they cannot measure up to His standard of loving, then it would be in your best interest to move on. God is a friend and a lover who thinks the best of you. He who would sacrifice the life of His own son for you, wants only the best for you. If someone does not value you like God values you, then your relationship is destined for trouble.

When we get away from the crowd and devote some time alone with Him, He treats us like royalty. When you discover God, you discover loves true character. One moment in time with Him, can change our whole outlook on life. We can discover who God created us to be. When we discover just how precious we are to Him, it becomes our responsibility to treasure and honor God's creation by how we allow others to treat us. When we require better, then we receive better. To be a conduit of God's love, with it freely flowing in and out of us, we must be both *giving* it and *receiving* it. We must *require* love, to *receive* it.

Today's Reflection:

In today's reflection, consider how you have loved yourself over the years. Does it reflect the same way God loves you? Are there times you have denied yourself love? If so, what do you think contributed to this? If not, consider this, have you denied love to others who needed it? Journal your answers below.

_____

_____

_____

_____

_____

_____

_____

_____

_____

_____

_____

_____

_____

_____

_____

_____

There's more to sex than mere skin on skin. Sex is as much spiritual mystery as physical fact. As written in Scripture, "The two become one." Since we want to become spiritually one with the Master, we must not pursue the kind of sex that avoids commitment and intimacy, leaving us more lonely than ever—the kind of sex that can never "become one." There is a sense in which sexual sins are different from all others. In sexual sin we violate the sacredness of our own bodies, these bodies that were made for God-given and God-modeled love, for "becoming one" with another. Or didn't you realize that your body is a sacred place, the place of the Holy Spirit? Don't you see that you can't live however you please, squandering what God paid such a high price for? The physical part of you is not some piece of property belonging to the spiritual part of you. God owns the whole works. So let people see God in and through your body.

1 Corinthians 6:16-20
The Message Bible

43

EMBRACING THE SILENCE...

*I*t is absolutely okay to not be in a relationship right now. It is a tragedy that millions of people spend their lives depressed and missing all the life God prepared for them to live. Singleness can be challenging around Valentine's Day, Christmas, birthdays, and New Year's Eve. Even worse, millions of people find it hard to sleep alone every single night. You may find yourself trying to fill an empty space in your soul while restlessly tossing and turning and clinging to pillows.

Still, those who are happily single have discovered something that the unhappy have not. They have discovered we are never truly alone. The Spirit of Love is always with us. Just because you do not have a physical, tangible representative of love does not mean that the Spirit of Love is not with you. Finding God, means finding Love. When we truly find Love, we learn that Love has the ability to be embodied in *any* person. That includes you.

Being alone can be tough because of the silence. Late at night, after the busyness of day, you are alone with your thoughts and memories of past loves. You remember how good love felt. You remember how they smelled. You remember the way they touched you and made your toes curl. You remember walks in the park and late-night dinners. You even touch the pillow beside you remembering the whispers in the dark.

As you spend your nights dwelling on your love of the past, you ignore the Love calling out to you today. There is a love deep down inside you, eager to be embraced. The Love you are waiting to experience through another individual is already within you. And though you have not recognized it before, that Love is holding you through this storm. You do not have to deny yourself the right to live - waiting for something you already possess. So, lie back, exhale, pull the covers up, and fall in the arms of God's Love.

Today's Reflection:

In today's reflection, take some time to be silent in God's presence. During that time, meditate on the 4-letter-word LOVE. At first, you may naturally think about people you have loved like your spouse or significant other; or children and family members. But try to just focus on the word itself first. How have you typically defined love? Is it acts of service by others, gifts given to you, or maybe affirming words spoken about you? As you meditate on the word in silence, allow it to become a signpost leading you to the warmth of God's presence. Do this for about 20 minutes, or longer if needed. Then, think about how The Spirit of Love inside you feels. Journal your new love experience below.

_____

_____

_____

_____

_____

_____

_____

_____

_____

_____

_____

_____

_____

_____

For I know the plans I have for you," says the LORD. "They are plans for good and not for disaster, to give you a future and a hope.

Jeremiah 29:11

NLT

44

ALONE IN THE GARDEN...

*W*hen God created Adam, He created him alone. But it is not recorded that Adam ever got lonely. It is not recorded that he asked for a mate. It is not even recorded that Adam was afraid of being alone. Though Adam would meet the definition of alone *in our books*, Adam never realized he was alone. He was not hoping and wishing for a mate. In essence 'being' Adam is all he knew.

Adam went about the busyness of the day, tending to the garden as God created him to do. He was busy naming animals. As he took walks in the cool of the day talking to the Father, He never knew the concept of *alone* or what feelings were associated with it - Adam was content. If we are to be happy while in our singleness, we must arrive at this place.

Our society, with its television shows, movies, and seductive music, images are portrayed that suggest we must be intimately connected to another human to feel complete. We get the idea we must either find a mate, or find ourselves doomed to a lifetime of lonely days and nights. This false perception instills in us a fear and anxiety about being alone. As a result, we jump into relationships too soon and with the wrong people. When we are deceived by the world we see around us, we fear missing out. Waiting for God's best becomes a daunting idea.

If it were not for the false realities portrayed by the media, we would enjoy our days and rest peaceably at night content with the Love of God.

We'd be naturally focused on our relationship with our Creator and the work we have been created to do. We would take walks in the cool of the day - enjoying inspiring conversations with Him. We would hardly ever entertain the idea that we are *alone*. Adam did not know that woman would arrive soon. As he focused on *being*, God himself determined the time and place where his mate would be created.

God has an assignment for your life. And in His divine will and timing, He will surely reveal the mate for you to have and to hold. But there is no reason for you to fear separation from Love. Love has always been and always will be *in you*. While waiting for your change to come, enjoy your walks in the cool of the day. Focus on God and enjoy the sound of His voice. He created you for something great!

Today's Reflection:

Many divorced (*and some married*) couples will agree that a relationship is not a viable defense against loneliness. Despite your relationship status, it is still imperative that we find time to be alone. That alone time is crucial to our ability to maintain a relationship with our Heavenly Father. In today's reflection, describe how you approach alone time. Do you go cheerfully? Or do you approach alone time like you are being punished to isolation?

_____

_____

_____

_____

_____

_____

_____

_____

_____

_____

_____

_____

_____

My response is to get down on my knees before the Father, this magnificent Father who parcels out all Heaven and Earth. I ask Him to strengthen you by His Spirit—not a brute strength but a glorious inner strength—that Christ will live in you as you open the door and invite Him in.

Ephesians 3:14-16

The Message Bible

WE'VE GOT COMPANY!

*Y*ou are not alone. Once we have that fact settled in our minds, then we will no longer have to worry about being *left* alone. No matter who exits from your life, you will never be alone. No matter who rejects you, you are not alone. No matter what challenges you may be facing – whether job loss, death of a loved one, or dreams shattered – you are not alone. In all of this you still have value.

So, let us take advantage the opportunity to experience all that life has to offer. There comes a point in time where we must become comfortable and satisfied with the company of our Creator. He stands and knocks at the door of our hearts. He's waiting on the doorstep of our lives for us to welcome Him in. He is not a salesman waiting at the door with gimmicks. He's not coming to take anything away from you. And He is surely not here to do a survey. But He is standing there patiently, waiting for us to invite Him in to begin a lifetime of intimacy. He's here and He is ready to start an eternal relationship. Can you hear Him? He knocks lightly at the door? He's not banging and demanding to come in. But God gently taps at our hearts asking us to grant Him permission to come in and love on us.

Far too often, we have gotten dressed and set the table for someone else. Why do we give the love, time, and attention that God deserves to others? He's always there – gently tapping at the door. Even after others reject and abandon us, He's gently tapping – ready to listen when we are heartbroken and disappointed. We have delivered first-class service to the people and careers we thought were good for us. But now, it is time to make God our priority.

We open our hearts quickly when new opportunities arrive at our doorstep, ringing the bell to come in. When they arrive, our home smells good, expensive candles are lit, dinner is done, and the wine is chilled. They always arrive when things are *good*. But after a while, we discover they only had temporary pleasure to offer. They blew out the candles and ate all the steak. The pie is all gone, and the wine bottle is empty! They have taken you for everything good you had to offer and left you to clean up the mess! You may be tired, disappointed, and hopeless. But still, again there is a gentle knock at the door. Again, we have company. God still stands on the other side gently tapping, and He's got His own wine. This time—*let Him in.*

Today's Reflection:

You know how you treat visitors who are visiting you for the very 1st time? You treat them with the best of service, right? Then, you know how you treat those who have been to see you *many* times. They have earned your trust. So, you welcome them in and tell them, make yourself at home, right? They know their way around your place well and tend to stay around longer. How many times have you welcomed God into your heart? Do you still treat like a fist time visitor or has He now earned your trust enough to stick around as long as He likes? Journal your answer in today's reflection.

_____

_____

_____

_____

_____

_____

_____

_____

_____

_____

_____

_____

_____

_____

God can do anything you know—far more than you could ever imagine or guess or request in your wildest dreams! He does it not by pushing us around but by working within us, His Spirit deeply and gently within us.

Ephesians 3:20
The Message Bible

A CALL TO ACTION:
DANCE WITH LOVE...

*G*et up and dance! Did you come to life's party just to stand on the wall? The life you are waiting to live, is passing you by. You may have your eye on someone you would like to dance with. I know you are waiting for them to ask you to join them. But are you going to wait all night? Be bold! Be brave! Get up and move towards the floor all by yourself. At least give it a try. Don't be afraid of who's watching. Some may think you are silly. But most will wish they had the courage. Many are dancing with someone just to be dancing. They just could not bear the thought of dancing alone.

Life is playing a song that everyone loves to hear. The tempo is fast at times but then slower other times. Sometimes things are nice and easy. Other times we can just barely keep up. When you hear the beat of life, everything in you wants to get up and move. Things will not always work out the way we want them to. But finding the right partner is key. Choose your partner wisely. Your hearts must hear the same song to dance gracefully and in harmony with one another. But the harmony is dependent upon two hearts beating as one. When you get up and begin to move your body to the rhythm of life - as soon as your feet hit the floor - *Love* will meet you there.

Dancing to life's rhythm brings all the peace, joy, and liberty you could imagine. You move as the Spirit calls you to move and stand when it tells you to stand. Life is not always so fast paced, so you slow down and breathe when the tempo is slower. But when things change quickly, keep your eyes fixed on your partner. Trust and know that the Spirit will guide you and anoint you with the wisdom to make the right decisions. All you need are the guts to move. But when you get to life's dancefloor, let Love take the first step. You may not have a spouse, a mate, or child right now. But for now, just dance with Love. He is all you need. *Selah*

Final Reflection:

You did it! You have just completed 45 days of healing, recovery, and discovery. Now, it's time for your personal reflection. In this final reflection, take a glance back on your condition at the beginning of this devotional. Overall, how are you different after these past 45 days? What questions did you have for God that you now have answers to? What hurts have been healed? What voids have been filled?

_____

_____

_____

_____

_____

_____

_____

_____

_____

_____

_____

_____

_____

_____

_____

_____

_____

COURAGE TO TRUST LOVE AGAIN

ho said that you weren't fit for love? Who said it was all your fault? Who said you weren't the right size, or the right shape? Who said you had to have a huge wedding? Who said that you didn't deserve to marry again? Who said you deserved to be left alone? Who said God wouldn't love you after going through a divorce? Who said you can't start the business again? Who said you couldn't earn a degree? Who said you wouldn't eventually succeed?

Get delivered from people. Once you get past what you have heard people say about you and your situation, then you can begin to hear God tapping at the door. The enemy's trick is to keep you so distracted and so confused that you can't hear Him asking to come into your heart. Doubt is like a thunderous tornado in your soul. As you struggle to clear your mind, the lies of doubt are repeated louder and louder and you are driven in circles. You rehearse what happened over and over in your mind; what *they* did, what *you* did back, and how you wish you could have done things differently.

But God wants you healed. He wants you whole. He wants you happy and secure in Him. When people abuse us, they want us to fear living a life without them. They likely have suggested you would never find another love – *better than theirs*. When people abandon and leave us for dead, they dare us to get up again. As long as God lives, there is *always* a better love. It is the relationship with Him after all that counts.

We may fear trying love again, because we fear that it will not work. Still, so what if it doesn't work? If it works - it works. If it does not - then it doesn't. Failed relationships do not mean you should deny yourself the opportunity to experience love again, no matter the outcome. After 10 years of marriage, and left single with 3 children, I was sure that I'd be forced to live the rest of my life alone. My heart was shattered. Dreams of the happily ever after were gone and destroyed. Nothing in me believed that God could possibly give me another chance at love. I thought, "Who would want me and 3 teenagers?" So, like a prisoner, I gave up on the idea of remarriage. I committed my life to my children, my career, and my ministry. Unbeknownst to me, I would begin to discover my own worth again.

In my singleness, I would find out that all the things I wanted to do with someone else, God wanted to do with me. All the love I wanted to feel at the hands of man, I learned that God wanted to touch my wounded areas Himself. So, after 3 years of being separated from my ex-husband, I finally filed for a divorce. I finally decided to pursue a new life. Once I made up my mind to pursue freedom and forgave him and myself, the court process was pretty smooth and quick.

Soon, after it became final, I began having dinner dates with Love. The mere idea of Love was all I needed to begin. Love helped me buy a really nice car for myself. Love took me shopping and showed me how to dress like I was well kept by "The King". I learned to choose quality in all things over quantity. Love taught me to choose to go places and do things that would emanate the inner joy I had inside all along.

Instead of feeling naked and insecure about ordering a table for one and one ticket to the show, I began to walk through the doors of life holding my head high and smiling. I had a new bounce in my walk. I did not have to wait for someone to come along and take my arm to validate me. I was already well-kept in the arms of God. I didn't have to wait for someone else to get ready. Nor did I have to compromise what brought me joy for what someone else wanted instead. I did not have to spend the evening impressing anybody, because Love taught me (dressed up or dressed down) I am lovely - just the way I am.

My confidence soon grew strong and the peace that resonated from within me became attractive to others. When you finally embark upon the love that is resting inside you, you soon discover that you already have everything you need or desire. The love, the acceptance, the validation, the status—its *aaaaalllllll* inside! You also discover that there is nothing this world can offer that you don't already have. Now that truth alone is a rewarding concept.

Yet even with my new liberated way of thinking, I would soon find myself asking the Father again for a mate. After a short while, I was approached by what seemed to be what I had been praying for all along. I thought, "Now I've found someone who is equally yoked and has his own relationship with the Father. Finally, someone who would understand my worship, my walk with God, and my calling in life to serve."

Even though I felt this would be the one, I was afraid. I was afraid to trust love again. I remember thinking, "I've already been rejected, abandoned, and left to gather the shattered pieces of my heart." When you feel like the rug has been snatched from underneath your feet, it can be difficult to find your secure footing again. Furthermore, once I found my security in God – I had no desire to place myself in a position to be hurt again. I now understood what love felt like and I didn't want anything less.

So, one day at a time, I carefully let down my walls and trusted love again. I prayed long and hard about the relationship, asking God to show me if he indeed would be the one. Reminded that God would never leave me nor forsake me, I slowly cracked the door open and let love tiptoe into the living room of my heart.

I honestly believed that this guy carried the Spirit of Love which indeed blessed me. Finally, I felt as if I were receiving a physical touch from God. Unfortunately, somewhere along the way, his hidden motives were revealed and after nine months of courtship my heart wound up broken again. Devastated and suffering from depression, I didn't want to see the light of day. I felt lifeless, confused, and cheated. I trusted him, *and* I trusted God. I blamed myself thinking, "How could I allow this to happen again?" The negative self-talk ensued, and I started beating myself up for letting my walls back down. I even questioned, "After all I have been through, how could God allow me to go through this again?"

The tears and depression continued for several months - my spiritual mother and closest friends called me around the clock. It was as if they had agreed to rotate shifts checking in and praying for my deliverance from the snare of depression I found myself in. Then, suddenly, when I least expected it – I felt the spirit moving again. I could hear the rhythms of life in my ears, and my once emotionally paralyzed body felt the urge to dance. I was finally convinced that there was still life worth living after heartbreak.

Now, I know for sure, that God will allow us to experience hurt temporarily. But, He only does this to draw us closer to Him. It is natural to expect God to shield us from all forms of hurt. If He did this, we would never have a mature knowledge of just how much we need Him. If our hearts are never broken, they remain calloused and closed. God would have no point of entry to fill us with His love. He could never influence our lives.

Soon, I began feeling fresh life breathed inside of me. I began to see the clouds move away and the sun began to shine in my life again. I felt the arms of Love wrapped tightly around me. If I struggled to sleep in the silence of the night, Love would gently rock me to sleep. The tears had stopped flowing and the spirit of heaviness was lifted from my heart. I was ready to move on. I was ready to live again. I arose from my bed of despair, put on my dancing shoes, and headed to the dance floor.

I had made up in my mind "never again." This time I would be more careful and allow God to be the guard standing at the door of my heart. I believed His hands are the safest place for its protection. We are all human and prone to make mistakes. We are all capable of dropping the ball. So, never again would I task someone with a job so critical: protecting *my heart*. Once I placed my heart in God's hands, I discovered just how delicately He catered to me. I realized that in His hands is where it belonged all along. Consequently, I made a life-altering decision. I resolved that's where my heart will stay.

Now this does not mean that I've quarantined myself and locked intimacy out. It does, however, mean that even within the confines of a great relationship, my heart belongs to God. Essentially, *both* our hearts will belong to Him. See, when both our hearts are devoted to the Father, then He can occupy the voids and repair the breaches that have been created by painful experiences. We cannot avoid the healing process.

As a result of our surrendering to God's call for an intimate relationship with Him, we will cease to expect our partners to fill that empty space. In God's presence, we are filled with the love needed to become and remain whole. Individual wholeness is critical to the success of any intimate partnership. All of us – single, married, divorced, engaged, widowed, etc. – *must* devote our hearts to our Creator. That is the only defense we have against its ruin.

I've grow to enjoy dancing happily alone with Love—until He orchestrates someone to join us in this dance. I've realized that I don't need to fill the space with another partner. My healthy boundaries are intact, and I have granted God the key to the door of my heart. Nobody is coming in to take my steak and potatoes again! Nobody will drink all my wine again! This joy that I have, Love gave it to me. Little did I know; real Love meets me on the dance floor of life every time I feel the urge to move.

God, who is *Love*, was resilient. He worked hard every day to gain my trust – even though I worked even harder to keep the doors shut. Still, day after day, Love tapped gently and patiently waited for me to invite Him in. Finally, God asked me, "Do you have the courage to get over what has happened in the past and accept what I am doing in your life right now? Or will you allow a *past* disappointment to cause you to miss out on all the Love I am trying to release in your life *today*?"

Scared out of my mind, I asked God for the courage to trust love one more time. "Just one more time Lord!" Everything I saw and felt seemed so real. However, when your vision is distorted by past hurt, it's hard to believe what you see with your own two eyes. With continued prayer, spending quality time alone with Him, and growing more confident at the sound of His voice - day by day I moved closer to the door. When I finally got the courage, I wrapped my fingers around the knob, turned it gently, and opened it. Just as God had promised, authentic Love was standing in front of me—holding his own bottle of wine!

AFFIRMED BY HIS LOVE

10 Noteworthy Characteristics of God's Love

1. God's Love is never disengaged.
This means He doesn't check out on us. He is not emotionally detached. The sacrifice of Jesus Christ created a bond that can never be broken. There is no hurt, sorrow, or shame with which He cannot identify. He knows just how we are feeling and will always empathize with us.

2. God's love never abandons- it is always present.
God's love does not disappear or ghost us when times get hard. Contrarily, that's when we can feel His presence the most. He is right there with us when we celebrate our victories as well as when we find ourselves on the brink of destruction. Even when we can't feel His presence, we can trust and know that we are not alone.

3. God's love is never hidden.
God gave us a roadmap to find His love – the Bible. And when we read the Bible, it shows us the way towards Him – prayer. When we live our lives chasing after God in prayer and worship – we can always find Him.

4. God's love is not insecure.
One thing God will never be is: unsure of how He feels about us. God knew exactly what He was doing when He sent His son to die for us and He knew why. He didn't second guess or doubt that we were worth His best sacrifice. So, don't worry He will never come back like an Indian giver and to reclaim it. His love is yours for all eternity!

5. God's love keeps its promises.
God cannot lie. With that in mind, we can rest each night assured that no matter how turbulent the storm becomes, He will not allow a hair on your

head to be lost. His love promises that, as long as we keep the King in our hearts, we will never be separated from Him – whether were on the mountaintop or in the valley. Nothing you can do will ever change His mind – a promise is a promise. God's love always delivers.

6. God's love is abundant.

There is more than enough of God's love to go around. He doesn't love one of us more than the other. On top of that, God's love knows no bounds, it is not capped or limited. Even when we fall short, He keeps on giving. We can never *earn* God's love anyway, so He just pours it out freely on us without stopping.

7. God's love is complete.

You cannot add anything to God's love to make it greater. Nothing can make God's love more valuable. It stands on its own, full of power. His love has enough power to chase us, heal us, deliver us, provide for us, protect us, restore us, affirm us, liberate us, and whatever else you need Him to do. Everything you need for healthy living can be found in God's love.

8. God's Love is liberating.

No matter what chains you find yourself in (mental, physical illness, emotional, unforgiveness, abandonment, rejection, relational, financial, etc.), God is the one who shows up ready to emancipate you. If you ever find yourself bound to anything—God's love is the only key to freedom. His love is the key that unlocks unconditional and eternal freedom.

9. God's love always heals & binds up our wounds.

First comes rest, then comes healing. When we are wounded spiritually and emotionally, it is imperative that we first find rest from our struggle. He draws us into His presence, filled with tears and sorrow, so that we can begin to rest in Him. Then the love of God will comfort us and begin the process of healing. As He comforts us, He then begins to heal the broken

places in us. His love saturates our souls and bandages our heart injuries –
so that healing can begin. This way we can be brought back to a place of
pure worship.

10. God's love is resilient.

God does not quit. He is always pursuing us. Our Heavenly Father always
believes in us and wants the best for us. It is His heart's desire to see us
living our filled with you – inside and out. Even when we have gone astray
a time or two *(or 50)*, His love will keep believing and wanting the best for
us. We can never be disqualified from receiving His love. For that reason
alone, we have what it takes on the inside to keep getting up after every
fall. We have a resilient spirit at work in us. It's Him! It's God! It is His
resilient Love on the inside of us that causes us to resurrect after every
breakdown. His resilient Love is like our internal engine, propelling us
forward into our destiny. So as long as He keeps getting up –as long as He
keeps loving – then we must follow.

OTHER TRANSFORMATIVE BOOKS
BY KIMBERLY MICHELLE FORD

THE CORE
It's All Inside!!!
Find it at www.Amazon.com

HOPE FOR THE SOUL
Make Yourself at Home In God's Heart
Find it at www.Amazon.com

THIRSTY SOUL
Finding Rivers of Living Water
Copyright 2019
Find it at www.Amazon.com

RESTORED SOUL
Getting to the High Place
Find it at www.Amazon.com

Share your reading experience!
Will you help me to be a blessing to others?
Please leaving a favorable book review on www.Amazon.com.

ABOUT THE AUTHOR

$\mathcal{M}$inister Kimberly Michelle Ford, a native of Atlanta Georgia, has committed her life to helping individuals heal and recover from abuse. She is committed to teaching survivors how to recover and maintain a life of freedom as a result of her own personal experience with sexual and domestic abuse. In 2007, Kimberly released her autobiography, "The Core: It's All Inside." In her debut book, she ministers to all who have suffered from the effects of sexual abuse, domestic violence, homelessness, and absentee parents. She recognizes that these are issues that far too many of us have encountered. In 2017, she founded My FreedomSoul, LLC – an outreach ministry aimed to support childhood trauma and domestic violence recovery. Through published books, small groups, outreach events and public speaking, the faith-based ministry's mission is to enrich the lives of survivors and victims' families. Kimberly works to erase the negative stigma associated with speaking out by applauding and rewarding survivors who have exhibited the courage to LIVE. This "champion" is passionate about empowering survivors of personal trauma to recover their freedom and celebrating their victory. In her own words: "Being an advocate for others is not merely about helping them to *get free*. Yet, advocacy involves demonstrating how to *stay free*. This little light of *mine* – I'm gonna let it *SHINE*! So, I pray that my courage to walk in total freedom, inspires you to pursue freedom too!"

~*Kimberly Michelle*

Connect with me:

Visit my website @ www.kimberlymichelleford.com
YouTube @RestoredToPower
INSTAGRAM @iamladykimberly
FACEBOOK @ KimberlyMichelle

Made in the USA
Columbia, SC
13 December 2024

49192845R00135